DIAMOND GEEZERS

Tough, transparent and trusted

Anthony Delaney

River Publishing & Media Ltd
Barham Court
Teston
Maidstone
Kent
ME15 6DF
United Kingdom

info@river-publishing.co.uk

ISBN 978-1-907080-15-9

Typeset by Richard Weaver
Printed and bound by
CPI Group (UK) Ltd, Croydon, CR0 4YY

contents

what other Diamond Geezers are saying ...

"This book is a must read for those of us who deep down long to grow into the kind of man that Jesus wants us to be. Written by a policeman who's become a pastor, it is honest, real, down to earth, wise and inspiring. I can't think of another book I've read that has motivated me so profoundly to embrace the Father's idea of redeemed masculinity. This really hits the back of the net. Buy it and read it!"
—**Dr Mark Stibbe**, author and leader of the Father's House

"In no-nonsense, power-packed language, Anthony Delaney shows how any lump of coal ('I'm just an old chunk of coal') can become diamond-brilliant if it will reflect a light that shines from within but is sourced from beyond – the Light of the World that enlightens every man (John 1:9) and turns 'dust is our fare' into 'diamonds are forever'."
—**Leonard Sweet**, bestselling author of *Jesus Manifesto* and *Nudge: Awakening Each Other to the God Who Is Already There*

"Anthony is a rare kind of man. He's a great leader, but he's honest about his weaknesses. He's a charismatic personality, but he's surprisingly self-effacing. He comes from an ordinary background, but has never settled for mediocrity. He's a strong man with a tender heart. In this excellent new book, Anthony speaks to every man who lives with the tests, conflicts, hopes and desires that crowd our daily lives. Anthony ably combines fresh insights with ancient truths to bring both an attractive invitation and a serious challenge

to find a new way to express authentic masculinity. This is a great book for a man like me – and probably a man like you!"
—**Mike Breen**, 3DM Global Team Leader

"Anthony has nailed it with this book. The way he tackles stuff head on, together with the themes he covers are just what us men need at this time. It will help us become the men we know we ought to be."
—**Carl Beech**, General Director CVM and founder of the Codelife movement

"Anthony Delaney is a diamond leader, excellent speaker and writer, and a wonderful father and husband. Read this book and give a copy to a friend!"
—**Andy Economides**, Director of Soteria Trust

"Ant's the real deal. A man's man who doesn't mince his words. His exciting new book is challenging, compelling, disturbingly honest and hard-hitting. I can't recommend it enough. It's an absolute belter!"
—**Steve Legg** (Sorted Magazine)

"My friend Anthony Delaney is genuine, gracious, gifted and a gentleman. This wonderful book brims over with his wisdom and wit. It will help you re-evaluate and refocus to remain faithful."
—**Canon J John**, The Philo Trust

"Anthony Delaney communicates in a way that is grounded in honesty, reality and integrity. He smashes every religious stereotype you've ever come across whilst remaining passionate about his faith. A beer, a Bible and a Balti shared

in the company of Anthony would be a great way to spend an evening."
—**Paul McGee** (the SUMO guy), bestselling author

"I'm lucky to have Anthony as a friend. This book reflects who he is: a Diamond Geezer. Sharp and transparent, tough on himself and candid towards others; passionate about his family. And if like lots of us you're fed up with modern society putting men down all the time, then read this. It will tell you, unashamedly, that it's great to be a bloke. This book will point you towards the pathway that will help you become the kind of bloke you secretly long to be – because this book isn't just choc full of theories – it's down to earth, practical, and deals with the kind of issues we need help with: fitness, finances, failures, family and fatherhood. So don't just stand there reading this – get the book. It could be the best choice you've ever made!
—**Eric Delve**, People without Limits

Dedicated to my wonderful daughter, Hannah,
who challenged me to write this ...

Thanks everyone!

Thanks to my beautiful wife, Zoe, for your continued encouragement to help me actually get finished and not just start another one. Your story and mine are one forever.

I'm so grateful for Emma and Ben and look forward to another righteous generation soon!

Thanks to Joel for helping me be a better Dad by being such a great son.

Thanks to John for being my best buddy. "That's the one!"

I'm grateful for the prayer and support of the staff and elders at Ivy Manchester, with whom it's such a great pleasure to partner with to see this city we love restored. Thanks to the whole church family for being such a bold, creative, diverse and loving community to belong to.

Special thanks to Andy Hawthorne for the foreword and to Ems Hancock, not only for checking through each chapter, but also, very helpfully, occasionally asking, "Did you really mean to write that?"

Finally, thanks to Tim Pettingale and to Jonathan Bugden at Integrity Media.

"No matter how diamond-bright your ideas are dancing in your brain, on paper they are earthbound."

—William Goldman

foreword

Everything about Jesus Christ and the Christian faith ought to appeal to men. Jesus was undoubtedly a man's man – his closest friends were working class guys with whom he ate, drank, partied and shared a message of sacrifice, power, and – ultimately – amazing joy. Surely men have got to appreciate that?

Yet the truth is that for the last few decades men have been voting with their feet and leaving the Church in droves – to the extent where there are now roughly twice as many women as men regularly attending church. This is disastrous news for anyone who wants to see the nation changed for the better, because the Christian Church should be at the heart of every community's transformation.

A large part of the problem in my opinion is one of leadership. My theory is that probably the worst possible route into Christian leadership is the one that so many take i.e. public school, Oxbridge, and then straight into theological college, often ending up leading airy fairy, irrelevant, slightly effeminate churches that ordinary blokes would pay good money not to attend.

This is clearly a bit of a caricature, and obviously it's not entirely a leader's fault if they are of good stock, have gigantic brains and are extremely out of touch. It is, however, a massive breath of fresh air to receive wisdom from a truly sharp guy, who grew up in Manchester's mean streets before spending several years as a Police Officer, pounding the beat on some of Europe's most deprived estates, witnessing some of the worst life has to offer, but never giving into despair. Instead, actually becoming more and more convinced that the good news of Jesus is utterly relevant to men, even in the most desperate of situations.

By the time Anthony did go to theological college himself, he had proved Christianity. Not just in oak paneled libraries or beautiful mural-decorated lecture rooms, but out where it really counts – on the front line. This is part of what makes *Diamond Geezers* such a compelling read, with its earthy wisdom, practical application and great stories. It's just what real men in today's confused world need.

Ant and I have been mates for several years, but since he and his family moved to Manchester a couple of years ago, we've actually got really close. We've drunk beer, watched sport and regularly laughed until we've cried together. Through it all, I've discovered one of the most genuine followers of Jesus I have ever come across. He really is a sickeningly great dad, husband, friend and leader, who heads up a fast-growing church that (for a change) lots of men want to be part of.

So read on. I know you will find *Diamond Geezers* funny, challenging and life-affirming. And like Anthony and I, you might even discover how amazing the ultimate man's man really is.

Andy Hawthorne
Founder and Director, Message Trust

A Diamond Geezer

"The true 'man of steel' has a 'heart of gold'"

—Mike Breen

ONE

show us what you're made of!

As I schoolboy, I remember the humiliation of standing on a freezing, hard soccer pitch in shorts that wouldn't fit me for the next five years. I hated football with a passion. I was *so* inept that nobody wanted me on their side. Longing for the game to finish so that I could thaw out my hands on the dusty white pipes inside, I tried my hardest to stay away from the ball. Despite my best efforts to keep out of the action, occasionally that ball would cruelly roll my way as the P.E teacher shouted, *"Delaney! Show us what you're made of!"*

I talk to men all the time – men just like you, men under pressure, feeling the heat. The truth is, us guys are under stress from all angles: from the fall-out of the sliding economy, the expectations of our families, and from the impossible stereotypes the media presents of what a "real" and "successful" man should be like. We feel compelled to strive towards our own unreachable goals, or the targets others set for us that we too often fail to meet. It's only afterwards that we realize they are pyrrhic victories, ruinous to our souls, relationships or character. Instead of being elated, we're deflated.

Wrestling inner doubts and strong temptations, outer struggles and "spare tires", we wonder why we even bothered.

It was considered "character-building" when, in the Police Cadets at sixteen, I was told to go out for a morning run across bitter mountainous areas, before breaking the ice off a stream and submerging myself in the sub-zero waters. No whimpering was permitted or press-ups were the punishment. *"Show us what you're made of!"* rang again in my ears. The only character trait such "jollies" developed in me was a reservoir of latent loathing for the sadists who dreamt them up.

Men can climb mountains or base jump to show that they are strong, resilient and manly. Dissatisfied with life as they know it, more and more men seek sexual conquests to prove they've still "got it". Trophy wives, bonuses or certificates on the wall may fill some of the emptiness, but never quite seem to plug the gap for long. So they try other things.

But can athletics, acquisitions or achievements really validate our manhood? Do we have to join a street gang or become a veggie to show that we're tough or sensitive or whatever we think a "real" man should be like?

The problem is, of course, all of the things we try are external. And nothing external shows what we are really made of. If we want to know what we are truly like, we need to look inside. Ask those who live closest to you, those who know you best, if you dare! Ask yourself. Who *is* the you that nobody else can see? What do you do when you are under pressure? What do you do when you feel the heat?

I want to be up front and say that I believe you also need to ask the God who made you. You will never understand yourself – your limitations and your potential – until you know what he made you of, and for.

For many men, the thought of belief in God or going to church is repulsive. Maybe that's how you feel. You are not alone. Over the last 20 years in the UK, 38% of believing men left the Church. For men aged under 30, nearly 50% left in the same period of time. A recent *Sorted Magazine* survey found that the vast majority of blokes would feel more comfortable in the lingerie section of a department store.

As a little boy I remember being made to go to a church service. As I knelt down at the front, where the sickly smell of incense was stronger, the priest smudged dirt and oil on my head and intoned, "Remember you are dust – to dust you shall return." Not a very nice thing to tell a six year old. I didn't understand it. Now I do. As a minister myself, I have stood at thousands of gravesides and realized that the mortality rate is still running at a hundred percent. Nobody gets out of here alive! I'm mortal and so are you. One day the atoms we are made up from – all those protons, neutrons and croutons – will return to dust and all that will remain will be whatever kind of legacy your decisions in life created, which will really show what you were made of.

So what do you see when you look inside? The premise of the rest of this book comes from the idea of two kinds of mineral, both made of carbon: Coal and diamond.

COAL MEN

A lump of coal can look quite big and impressive, pretty tough. But, put it under a bit of pressure and it will crumble. Expose it to heat and it will burn. It won't last. I know too often I have been like that: content with the outward show of looking like I've got it all together, but knowing inside it's a different story. Men are like that. Not just some men. Most.

To protect a vulnerable inner-self that wants to see ourselves as doing okay, we put on a show. We don't really know who we are, what it is to be a man, or what we want from life. But we know that there must be more than this.

Karl was convinced he had superpowers and could fly. He was always making some kind of wings or jumping off the prefab buildings at my Junior school. When you heard the ambulance siren, it was a safe bet he'd discovered gravity again! From the time we put on a cowboy outfit or climb somewhere high to test our superpowers, men become skilled at play-acting. We end up putting on a mask – a mask that says everything is happy and okay in my little world, inside of me, with my friends, with my family and my work. Occasionally something good happens which gives us a buzz or a taste of what we were really made for and that can keep us smiling or distracted for some time. But, whether we make the sale, get the girl or score the goal, eventually men ask, "Now what?" and settle back into the phony role-playing again.

Do you know why coal is black? The structure of the atoms in coal is such that it absorbs light of all wavelengths. If we're self-absorbed and we don't let anyone look at what's really going on inside us, we end up in darkness.

"Coal men" (no offense to anyone in the solid fuel delivery business) have perhaps never known the genuine love of a father in a way that they can understand and relate to. Therefore they are not able have good relationships with others. They don't begin to understand women and find it difficult to maintain lasting, healthy marriages. Their networks of friendships are often shallow, superficial and short-term. Coal men often end up with their wives divorcing them or their kids not talking to them. They throw themselves into their work to show themselves that they are successful somewhere, then die early from stress.

Coal looks impenetrable, but when you examine it close enough you can see it's actually full of holes. A coal man has nothing at his centre but emptiness. Isolated and lonely, he is always competing with someone he can never win against (i.e. himself). Emotionally stunted, he is never quite able to make the difference he would really like to in the world, because he would have to deal with his inner world first.

Some coal men are violent, aggressive, patriarchal, resentful, misogynistic or abusive, embittering their families and those they are supposed to love and protect. Others are new age luvvies trying to project sensitivity as the appropriate response to feminism's advances, but too weak and afraid of healthy conflict to be respected by women, or to bring the guidance and discipline that's actually required to be a good parent.

Coal men are *male*, but not *real men*. Look a little closer and you see the gaps. Our society is populated by anxious little boys who never grew up to attain the glorious maturity of maleness that is their true inheritance.

Sadly, men commit over 90% of all acts of violence. They comprise over 90% of the prison population and 75% of the unemployed. Tragically, far too many, tired of the outward show and the emptiness of their hearts, decide the best decision they can make is to step out of this life sooner rather than later. Suicide is a leading of cause of death among young men. Men commit suicide four times more frequently than women. From my intake year at secondary school alone, I can think of five men who never saw their thirties because they topped themselves. They never got to fly, never fulfilled their dreams.

Coal men, whether the hard and scary or soft and wimpy variety, have a very tough time getting married (because of fear of commitment) and an even harder time staying married (because of failing to do what they said they were committed to). They are stuck in front of the TV or computer, or stifled in jobs they don't find meaningful. They get into debt for pastimes that don't satisfy or to buy things to impress friends they are not close to. They wade through life, digging deeper and harder, but they never fill their internal void.

If as a man you tell me that none of this connects with you at all, you are in denial. Someone may have given you this book for a reason! Years of policing and pastoral experience have shown me that I am not talking here just about extreme cases. Endless talks in the pub, men's events, retreats and counseling sessions tell me that this is the unspoken truth for the vast majority of men in our society – and that it's getting worse with every new generation.

The reality is this: most men, despite what the outward indications show, if you put them under some kind of pressure, will crumble one way or another. Pick up any paper today and you'll be able to read the stories of the coal men: vaunted sporting heroes hang their heads in the gossip column because they can put it in the net, but can't keep it in their pants. Business tycoons and politicians go under for not resisting that shady deal. Integrity and reputations lie in tatters, families in ruins. Is this the best our society can offer as role models for its boys?

DIAMOND GEEZERS

I'm certainly not a perfect man. I'm just an ordinary bloke who's found a few amazing truths along my journey. But I believe there is a better way for us to live passionately and positively – as a perfect man (under construction!)

A guy once came up to me at the end of a seminar I was leading in a huff. Do you know what his problem was? He didn't like my use of the term "bloke". Honestly! If, like him, you are that easily offended, I urge you to put this book down right now and go and get one that teaches you how to do cryptic crosswords or something. Oh … and get a life! I've written this as a bloke to other blokes and at times I may be blunt in my efforts to be practical.

You may disagree at times with what I say, but don't dismiss anything out of hand, even the stories about Bible characters I'll use throughout. Because the Bible is not just a good book, it is THE book. It's the most honest book in the world because it tells the stories of its characters warts and all. Even if you don't believe in God yet, believe that I believe God has a great plan for you, a better purpose than you ask for or dream up. He knows exactly what you're made of and he sees your value and potential. In fact, the heat and the pressure of life are His tools to shape you and your life into something better and brighter.

God doesn't want you to be a coal man. They are ten a penny in our society. He wants you to be a Diamond Geezer! We all know that true diamonds are so rare that they are incredibly valuable. Did you know that the process of diamond-recovery sifts out 180 million parts of other material to yield just one-part diamond? They require a lot of work in order to make them look as they do. Diamonds are not brilliant to look at when they are first found. They can be cut in many ways and the cut greatly impacts how they shine. If a diamond is cut poorly, it will be less luminous and may even be permanently damaged.

I don't want to waste your time. I've decided to cut this particular gemstone six ways, keeping it simple rather than complex. The chapters that follow are about vital issues that will be challenging for every man and every family. They stand alone as tests of clarity and quality, so you might be tempted to skip straight to one that interests you immediately. I know that's what most men do when they read any book, but I think on this occasion it would be better if you didn't. It's important to check out all the sides of this stone. Perhaps you could hold a "Geezers Group" meeting together every week or so, for the next seven or eight, with some other blokes to discuss the ideas together?

When I read a book, I find it helps to grab a highlighter and scribble on the pages, and make notes on the back pages. Feel free to disagree, but engage with the book, and be a committer not a quitter. I know how easy it can be to start a book and not finish it! Don't do that, please. Much of what I'm saying only hangs together at all because of what comes later in the book.

Remember, a diamond is basically still carbon, but deep in the Earth's mantle, hundreds of miles below the surface, it has been formed under high-pressure, high-temperature conditions. The process is such that its nature is changed, impurities disappear, and it becomes transparent and reflective, rather than self-absorbed. The closer you examine its luster, the more you see that something wonderful and precious shines from within. What matters is what's at the centre.

Being a Diamond Geezer means living gloriously as a man, the way you were created and meant to live, with nothing to prove, nothing to hide, and everything to live for.

I will talk about the details of all of this later on, but you can see from the diamond diagram throughout that I believe you will never fulfill your potential as a man without Jesus. The most important part of my life as a Diamond Geezer is knowing Jesus Christ and having a relationship with God at the very centre of my world. You may notice I didn't put the word "faith" there, tempting though it was to make everything start nicely with the same letter (a preacher's dream!) I want to help you see that it's not just faith, but *faith in Jesus Christ* that is the true centre we need to live out from. Nothing and nobody else can be a substitute for him. Everything else flows from that faith relationship. The Bible talks about the importance of the heart as the very core of your being, and while we will look at physical fitness, it's not speaking physiologically when in Proverbs 4:23 it says *"Above all else guard the heart for it is the wellspring of life."*

I want to demonstrate why having God at the centre of your life is the best possible foundation for a man's life. It affects all the other areas because real change only happens from the inside out. What is at the centre of your life right now? It could be your football team or your family or your finances. None of those are, of course, bad in themselves (unless it's Manchester City), but they are not meant to be the axis you base everything else around. Try to live with any of those things at the centre and you'll crumble when the heat is on.

Difficulties with health, parenting, screwing up at work are just symptomatic of the hole we men have in our hearts. We can pretend this doesn't apply to us, put on a happy face or make a show of bravado. But when the heat is on and the pressure comes, it isn't how much you can bench press but what is in the centre that matters most. It has been said that we are like a tube of toothpaste: when we get squeezed what is on the inside comes out. It has also been said that we are like a tea bag: we're not much good until we have been through some hot water!

The real journey of becoming a man is the journey that takes us toward becoming like THE perfect man. And while you might admire a sports or a movie star, I believe that throughout history there is no contender for the title of "perfect man" other than the Lord Jesus Christ.

The other facets around the diamond shape are all to do with your decisions, your actions and attitudes. If I was to sit down one-to-one with you and look you in the eye, as I have with many guys over the years, and ask you some questions relating to these areas, you would see how they are linked and intertwined.

What if I was to ask you some deep questions about how you have coped with life's inevitable *failures*?

How would you assess yourself as a *family* man – as a son, a sibling, a parent or a husband? (Maybe it would be better to get your kids or your wife in the room and ask them to rate you!)

Men in our society have been radically "under-fathered" for generations. How you relate to your earthly father is probably the single biggest determinant of your psychological health as a man.

When I joined the Police force I ended up working with men who I knew would die for me if necessary and vice versa. I still maintain strong friendship, many years on, with those guys. True friendship is not a slap on the back or a drink in the pub. Does anybody know your heart, your secret thoughts, what makes you laugh, what makes you cry, what makes you mad? Would your friendships last under pressure and under heat?

Many men are lazy slobs. Others become body obsessed to the point of idolatry. I maintain a good level of *fitness* for my age by going to the gym regularly and training for the occasional half marathon. I want to be fit for purpose, to steward my body well and be able to give the best that I can give to everything I do.

If I asked you questions with regards to your *finances*, how would you respond? Your bank statement says everything about your priorities. What would true financial freedom and balance mean to you – according to the Bible's time-proven wisdom? It will be very interesting to look at that together later in the book. You're in for a few surprises.

You know what I think? Unashamedly? It's great to be a man! I love being a bloke, with loads of mates younger and older who are becoming real men – the way God wants them to be: men who love to laugh, men who love their wives, men who are strong and yet compassionate, men who pray and act with courage, men who are great in any kind of relationship, men who become great dads, great husbands, great men and great men of God.

SOCKS AND SANDALS AND SEXUAL SCANDALS

The stereotype of a Christian man turns our stomachs. It's repulsive (the opposite of attractive, as the droves of men who have left the Church in Britain in recent decades testifies). A BBC poll said men think church is for "wimps, women and weirdos", and sadly that picture is all too often true. It's not surprising so many men in our society don't want to cross the threshold of a church building when it's full of other men who look like they are busy posing for their passport photographs.

There is something far better for you than that. Having Jesus at the centre of your life doesn't mean God wants you to be a weedy, Bible-punching, religious nutter. He doesn't want you to lead a double life where you just add a religious mask for Sundays to all the other masks you own. That just leaves you feeling ashamed and alone, having let yourself down and everybody else who depended on you. He wants to give you a cause worth sacrificing for, a battle to win, and brothers to fight alongside you in the war for your own soul.

He wants to shape you to be like Jesus. He wants to make you a Diamond Geezer!

Years ago, a man used to carve fantastic stallions and sculpt them. Somebody asked, "How is it that you can take these lumpy old pieces of wood that are full of splinters and knots and make such beautiful horses from them?"

"Easy," he replied. "I hold them up to the light, I see the stallion inside, and I cut away everything that isn't horse."

In the 1800s, Baptist preacher Charles Spurgeon said, "There has got abroad a notion, somehow, that if you become a Christian you must sink your manliness and turn milksop." No way! God wants to take you on a journey throughout your life where he will use pressures and heat to transform you. Sometimes he may cut away things you wish he would leave well alone. Sometimes he will be very gentle and patient. But the Bible promises that if you put yourself in his hands, God will shape you in various areas, if you let him and cooperate with him, so that one day when you see the only perfect man, Jesus Christ, you will find that you know him, because you will be like him.

My spiritual father and former ministry partner, Eric Delve, is fond of reciting the following poem by Henry F. Lyte (who wrote the famous hymn *Abide With Me*). It illustrates the process of Diamond Geezer formation very well. Read it aloud if you can and if you don't understand it now, one day you may.

Whom God Chooses

When God wants to drill a man,
and thrill a man, and skill a man,
When God wants to mould a man,
To play the noblest part;
When he yearns with all his heart
To create so great and bold a man,
That all the world shall be amazed,

Watch his methods; watch his ways.
How he ruthlessly perfects
When he royally elects!
How he hammers him and hurts him
And with mighty blows converts him
Into trial shapes of clay
Which only God understands;
While his tortured heart is crying,
And he lifts beseeching hands!
How he bends but never breaks
When his good he undertakes.
How he uses whom he chooses,
And with every purpose fuses him;
But every act induces him
To try his splendor out -
God knows what he's about!
Go then, earthly fame and treasure!
Come disaster, scorn, and pain!
In thy service, pain is pleasure;
With thy favor, loss is gain.
I have called thee, Abba, Father;
I have stayed my heart on thee.
Storms may howl, and clouds may gather;
All must work for good to me.

The word diamond comes from a Greek word that means "unbreakable". Are you ready to come with me on the journey towards that true inner and outer strength? Stop chipping away at life from the outside. Learning to live your life from the inside out, with Jesus at the centre, is not just the best way, but the ONLY way to be a real man in the world today!

Father
Fitness
Friends
JESUS
Finances
Family
Failures

> "If I'd known I was going to live this long, I'd have taken better care of myself."
>
> —Eubie Blake

TWO

Fitness

[fit for life]

I'm feeling good. I'm writing this mid-morning, feeling fresh. My mind is active and full of ideas. I have a positive attitude. I'm high on natural endorphins and I even smell nice. That's what putting yourself through a program of regular exercise can do. An hour ago I really didn't want to do the plyometric circuit (movements combining strength with dynamic jumps like squat thrusts), but while it's one of my toughest, sweatiest, workout sessions, I know it burns fat and provides power, balance, stamina and core stability simultaneously. The program I follow was designed by a former Royal Marine and tomorrow I'm scheduled for a middle distance run, the day after is a rest day. Can't wait for that!

I'm a doer rather than a spectator. Living in Manchester makes the odd visit to the "Theatre of Dreams" to watch United something of a must occasionally. I find I can't switch off and enjoy the match easily though. I detest being surrounded by men with huge beer guts shouting and swearing as they tell the athletes on the pitch how to play better. Years ago, as a Police Officer, I was put off the big league games. It became a place to arrest fighting idiots which wasn't much fun, though the overtime helped.

I have never been crazy about sports like football or cricket. Some guys are able to tell you the full line-up of every team, what the name of the manager was in 1971, and what brand of chewing gum he chewed. I have never had that kind of trivia lodged in my mind. My brain just doesn't retain that kind of stuff. I suppose that makes me a bit unusual. A lot of blokes I know have that information on the tip of their tongue. Not me. When I was at school the *only* sporting option was to play football. I was far from gifted at the game and was always pretty skinny for my age. This contributed to my lack of footie prowess in a school system where if you couldn't kick a ball you got kicked out of the way instead.

I recently heard *Tipping Point* author Malcolm Gladwell give a lecture. He speculated that the month of the year in which you are born makes a big difference as to whether or not you will be successful in sports. His belief is that it depends on the idiosyncrasies of the selection process used to identify and coach talent, just as much as it does on the athletes' natural abilities. It is all to do with where you are in the school intake year.

In one study of youth hockey professionals in his book *Outliers*, Gladwell postulates that since youth leagues determine eligibility by calendar year, children born on January 1st play in the same league as those born on December 31st in the same year. Because adolescents born earlier in the year are bigger and more mature than their younger competitors, they are often identified as "better athletes", leading to extra coaching and a higher likelihood of being selected for elite hockey leagues. He calls it "accumulative advantage".

That is now my excuse and I'm sticking to it.

"The first wealth is health."
—Ralph Waldo Emerson

I count myself pretty fortunate that at the age of sixteen I joined the Police Cadets and was immediately obliged to be part of all kinds of sports and workouts in the gym. Over the next few years I packed on weight and muscle and was soon able to knock people off the ball (or just over), even though my skills hadn't improved.

Since then I have been fairly disciplined in keeping myself fit. I have run marathons and mountain marathons as well as taking part in a number of short and middle distance triathlons. Even at the age of 45, I recently completed a half marathon in a personal best time. I'm not bragging, (well, maybe a bit!) but I discipline myself to exercise simply because I know it's easier to maintain rather than regain good health. I truly believe that looking after our bodies is not an optional extra or something those who have illnesses or problems need to do. Taking care of my body, for me, is something that is a major part of what my Christian faith calls "good stewardship – and stewardship is discipleship.

We're invited to remember in the pages of the Bible that everything we have – including our next breath and the lungs that receive it – is a gift from God. One day he will hold us to account for how we have lived. It matters to him how we treat everything we are given: money, family, job, the planet and of course our bodies.

One of the facets of our Diamond Geezer diamond is fitness. This may come as a surprise, especially if you were thinking that this is some kind of religious book.

But what if everything is spiritual?

What if all of our choices matter – even those connected to our health and wellbeing? I think these things are all interconnected.

There are two extreme camps that us men can fall into with regard to our bodies, fitness levels and general health. We can either deify or denigrate ourselves. Either we worship our reflection in gym mirrors whilst developing a six-pack, or we wallow before a TV screen drinking one.

The danger with worshiping your body is that it leads to pride. You don't have to be admiring your prowess on the treadmill or kissing your biceps to fall into this camp. Look at your checkbook or bank statement. How much do you spend on gym membership, suntans or even plastic surgery to defeat the signs of ageing (and the fear of death that is wrapped up in that)? Now, think about how much time, energy and money you put into your spiritual wellbeing. Do you do anything that feeds your inner being?

I'm forced to admit that in the past, when marathon training for example, I have put a big strain on family time and even neglected the people I love most. For what? A cheap medal or a t-shirt and the chance to prove something to myself? It is all about balance. I have learnt that the hard way.

Conversely, body neglecters don't struggle with pride but sometimes feel guilty instead. Maybe this guilt comes from other people telling them they need to shape up and change something in their lifestyle: stop smoking, drink less, get out more, put the console down and play a real game …

The neglecter responds, "It's my life. Who cares? Life's too short. I am going to die anyway! I'm not doing anyone else any harm." But living out this extreme does affect other people. Too many body-neglecters end up having to be cared for by the NHS or their families because they never took care of themselves.

At either extreme there will be tension with regards to relationships. To be brutally honest, either way it is caused by selfishness.

A husband hasn't seen his wife and kids all week because of the pressures at work. His game of golf is booked. Ignoring the pleas of his family, he throws his clubs in the boot. "I've been stressed out all week and I need to exercise now. You want me to be healthy don't you? I'm just looking after myself."

Another man sinks just one more cheeky beer, lights up another cig and turns the volume up to hear and cheer his team. His child wants to kick a ball in the park, but Dad responds, "Later son, I'm knackered."

What's God's perspective on how we treat our bodies? We're not the first to ask that question. The apostle Paul wrote about the issue to a group of believers in the city of Corinth:

> *"Do you not know that your body is a temple of the Holy Spirit, who is in you, whom you have received from God? You are not your own; you were bought at a price. Therefore honor God with your body."* (1 Corinthians 6:19-20)

When the New Testament was written, Greek philosophy and spiritual thought taught that what you did with your body didn't matter. Religion was seen as a purely spiritual thing with little or no bearing on our physical being at all. In the West today that Greek mindset prevails. One can only imagine how amazed the people at the church in Corinth were to receive this new teaching. Paul is saying that the God he serves and believes in cares very much about all aspects of life, from what we eat and drink to the way we look after our bodies.

The people at Corinth knew all about temples. The city was full of magnificent, holy sites for pagan worship for the pantheon of Greek gods. It must have been amazing for them to hear that this was just how God viewed their bodies: as temples, sacred sites that needed to be well-maintained since they were a place for deity to dwell.

But it's deeper even than that.

In the fourth century a Bishop called Athanasius was called in to adjudicate in a disagreement about who owned a particular boat. A man in Alexandria had made a boat by hand, painted it himself and knew every inch of it. One day he went to the port and it had been stolen! Because he loved that boat he scoured the nearby harbors, searching for it. The months turned into years until, by chance, he saw it one day near the Nile. It had been painted a different color, and had a new name, but he knew it was *his* boat! A long time had passed, however, and it had gone through several owners. The man who now possessed it had paid a fair price for it.

Athanasius decreed that the one who had made it would also have to pay the full price for the boat if he wanted it, saying, "Then nobody will ever be able to say that it doesn't belong to you."

God's perspective on our bodies is like this: they're not ours anyway – they're his.

Because my body is not "my body", I can't just do what I like with it – either to worship it (which is idolatry) or abuse it (which is sacrilege). God isn't just interested in the spiritual side of me, the whole package belongs to him. We have swallowed too easily the idea that there is a sacred and secular divide in life.

We belong to God because He created us in the first place, and then he paid the ultimate price to get us back so no one can ever say we aren't his. God wants a relationship with us. He doesn't just want us to know some things about him (like you might know some sporting facts – which I don't). He wants us to really *know* Him. Knowing God is not just about spending a hour or two with him on a Sunday.

And God wants to know us too. He is interested in what happens in your life throughout the week – of which looking after your body is a big part. It has a great deal to do with whether you will end up living what Jesus calls "life to the full" and it has a bearing on how soon you will get to experience the next life!

Resting heart rate of a fit man: 52 beats per minute
Time it takes a fit man to log eight million heartbeats: 30 years
Resting heart rate of a man who's out of shape: 72 beats per minute
Time it takes an out-of-shape man to log eight million heartbeats: 19 years

Your heart is a muscle and like any muscle that is exercised, it responds by getting stronger. Without exercise it will atrophy. As your heart gets stronger, your resting pulse rate will fall. Measures like this are more helpful than whether you feel healthy. Just because you feel okay doesn't mean you are healthy.

> **"We do not stop exercising because we grow old – we grow old because we stop exercising."**
> **—Dr. Kenneth Cooper (founder of aerobics)**

In one survey, 69% of men ticked the box that said they consider themselves "physically fit". Around 13% actually are. Fitness is, of course, something of a relative term. It's not just about lifting heavy weights, but comprises flexibility, strength and endurance. Fitness makes a difference to you emotionally, spiritually and intellectually. Fitness literally means "suitability". For a professional athlete it means being ready and at your peak on race day. Fitness for me means the ability to cope with what life throws at me and still having something in reserve. Can you work all day then be strong enough to change a wheel on the car or jog home? What are your energy levels like? A woman was asked, "Do you wake up grumpy in the morning?" She replied, "No, I let him have a lie in!"

I appreciate that some men reading this may have a disability or may not immediately be able to get into some high-level physical program. But speaking to the majority now: isn't it true you could maintain or improve your level of fitness if you were to start some form of program? I guarantee that the results will be more than physical. You will discover new levels of self-respect, determination and wellbeing. Couldn't you make a change for the better today in one of the three areas most important for fitness; exercise, correct nutrition and rest?

When I lived in Surrey I was inspired when I went to the local swimming pool and met soldiers who were plowing along the lanes. They had come from a local army rehabilitation centre. Headley Court is famous for the amazing work it does for young squaddies who have been injured in the war in Afghanistan or Iraq and who have come home to be rehabilitated. To see some of these men – double amputees and so on – not giving up, but pushing themselves to make the best of a terrible situation was so inspiring to me. They refused to just lie there. Many got involved in running marathons, doing things others would view as impossible, because they believed, "It's ain't over till it's over". So if you're a couch potato, what's your excuse? There may be a few things you can't do, but there are hundreds of things you can do.

WHAT FITNESS MEANS FOR YOU

I'm not saying you should let any kind of fitness program monopolize your life. Diamond Geezers don't go there. But any of us can set a goal and then push ourselves. To where? Beyond the limits of our expectations!

> **"If you always put limits on everything you do, physical or anything else, it will spread into your work and into your life. There are no limits – there are only plateaus – and you must not stay there, you must go beyond them."**
> **—Bruce Lee**

You must decide what fitness means for you, what you want to be fit for, and then how much time you can afford to spend on it. You don't need a crash diet or an impossible dream, you just need a purpose, a plan and program to follow for life. A plan to keep fit anywhere at any age with minimal time and equipment is achievable. Right now, thirty minutes of challenging exercise five days a week keeps me smiling, slim(ish) and sexy to my wife.

Your fitness aims are different to mine and I'm not going to try to design you a plan. But the most important parts about any fitness program are …

... to be honest with yourself – decide what's achievable
... to enjoy yourself – you are more likely to stick with it
... to challenge yourself – stretching your abilities will keep you from boredom
... to rest yourself – recovery is as important as training

BE SAFE

Of course, the first most important thing to do before embarking on any kind of fitness program is to see your doctor for a check up, especially if you are overweight, have high blood pressure (hypertension), any kind of irregular heartbeat or a history of any kind of medical condition that might affect your mobility. Go to a running shop to get correctly fitting shoes for your biomechanics so you don't get injured walking out of the door! Wear proper sports clothing to get yourself in the right state of mind from the start.

> "Pain is temporary. Quitting lasts forever."
> —Lance Armstrong

You have to start from where you are. Assess your level of fitness right now, then track your changes to stay motivated. Body fat scales are more helpful than normal scales, they calculate your BMI. Muscle weighs heavier than fat (there's another excuse for some of you), so while you get fitter and leaner you may not necessarily weigh less by following a fitness plan. Think about your diet, addictions to cigarettes, how much you drink and so on. There are various sites where you can predict your life expectancy based on your lifestyle now. Some of you need to do this quickly – it may mean you have to either make dramatic changes or read a lot faster to finish this book!

Many people I talk to seem to be under the impression that getting fit takes a long time. I don't think it does. You can see dramatic improvements from a regular and consistent workout pattern that only lasts thirty minutes a day, a few days a week, as long as you are working efficiently. I know that because I have seen it in my own life in recent years. I feel fitter now than I did fifteen years ago. I often exercise with a friend, Lindz West, who is a semi-professional football player ten years my junior (training with a partner is a great idea, but I sometimes wish I'd found a bloater instead).

What's your next step? Following a program with a mixture of resistance, exercises, stamina building, and aerobic fitness will give you that great feeling you only get as your body releases endorphins from exercise. You don't have to spend hours a day in a gym trying to get fit. Despite what a whole industry will say the contrary, you don't even need to join a gym! Whatever your age, whether you are fit or unfit right now, it's time to go to another level, and to do that you just need to learn the skills necessary to attain and maintain fitness then get on with it.

BE PREPARED

Baden Powell was right. It is important that we schedule regular workouts throughout the week and rest days too. Having a familiar routine will increase your chances to stick with it. 90% of success is just showing up – with your trainers on!

Find a time for exercise that suits you. It doesn't matter whether it's morning or afternoon or evening. Some people will say that it is good to train in the morning because testosterone levels are higher. None of that really matters. What matters is that you pick a time that works for you. This is true for prayer also!

Put your training kit together so you're ready to go. Don't put it off till tomorrow. Focus on now. You may feel like you can't be bothered, but if you have planned in your diary some time to train, then it's good to make a pact with yourself and say, "Whether or not I feel like doing it, I am going to start and keep on starting."

I find it useful to give myself occasional treats if I have not slipped away from my program, but have carried on with it, because what defeats a lot of us is that we don't see a difference overnight. It takes time to reach our goals. Consistency is important.

BE REALISTIC

You may not run the Marathon De Sables next year. You may not even want to carry on tomorrow. Remember, some days are harder than others. That's called life. As a runner I know that one day you will feel like you can run forever (believe me it will come) and other days you will feel like you are dragging the carcass of a dead moose up a hill. Don't give up.

Make sure you drink a lot of water, have a good low-fat diet and proper nourishment. Every health gain is worth the discipline it takes to achieve it. I used to smoke and though I know it's stupid and disgusting, I have to admit there are times when I crave a cigar. But do you know what? I crave a healthy life more. Say yes to the right things and no to the wrong things. Stick with it and you will see the results, and so will others.

"Step in da groove and move!"
—Bobby-Joe Edwards (light heavyweight boxing legend who goes to my church)

One of the spin-off benefits of exercise is that you will get happy. You will not go around looking like an extra from a Zombie movie all the time. So often, like today, I've finished an exercise regime feeling energized and motivated to get on with all the other things I have to do in life. I do all the other things I have to do better because I've put first things first. I find innovative thoughts for my work and creative ideas for my talks click into place almost out of nowhere as I'm running somewhere beautiful. Science has proven that exercise will reduce tension, depression and anger. Even twenty minutes can boost your mood for hours. If you become fitter your body will, in essence, detox itself. You will cut down on your cigarettes and bad habits not because you have to, but because you want to.

The Bible says you are *"fearfully and wonderfully made."* The human body has been designed by God as the pinnacle of his artistry. He created you to showpiece his glory, then paid the highest price imaginable to buy you back, so nobody can deny you belong to him. Therefore, honor God with your body.

Father
Fitness
Friends
JESUS
Finances
Family
Failures

"Success is the ability to go from failure to failure without losing your enthusiasm."
—Sir Winston Churchill

THREE

Failure

[let's get this one out of the way]

During the 2010 World Cup there were high hopes for the England team, but after a series of terrible performances they came back under a cloud with demands they be sacked – or at least hung, drawn and quartered! One headline I saw screamed, "You have let your country down". Everyone agrees: they should never fail like that. A) we invented the game in the first place and B) they are too highly paid and have been trained too much to fail to put a ball into a net a few times.

The fact is, we idolize success in our culture to such an extent that this kind of "failure" is almost the unpardonable sin. But people do fail nevertheless. Everyone. All the time.

We read every day about the failure of politicians, movie stars and sporting heroes. Closer to home, friends let us down; business partnerships fold because people let one another down; husbands fail wives, parents fail their kids, and kids fail to live up to the expectations of their parents.

Everybody fails. It is a great universal truth. We are all imperfect. Even successful people fail. In fact, if anything, successful people fail *more* because they try things more often and have to learn from their failures.

We will all fail often. It's not just a one off event! We cannot say, "I've learned now and I'll never fail again," because we will. None of us is perfect and so we fail and keep on failing until death stops us.

The big question then is: *how can we fail successfully?* How do imperfect people improve? How do we learn to move from saying, "I am a failure" to the more correct and healthy, "I have failed"? (Failure is an *event*, not a *person*).

People can be wrestled to the ground under the weight of failure – pinned to the mat by a fear of failing again. So they give up fighting and stop trying.

Fear of failure can cause us to be indecisive. Perhaps we can't make decisions or act on them, because we're afraid we're going to make the wrong move again.

Fear of failure can make you a workaholic, because it might all come crashing down any minute.

Fear of failure can make you a perfectionist. It's never quite right, you see; you're never satisfied.

Nobody wants to fail, but some people will do anything to win: lower their moral standards, try to cover up, blame someone else, or hurt people to hide their failures. Is there any way for us *not* to fear failure while not denying the consequences? Is there any way for imperfect people who break relationship with a holy God by breaking his commandments and his heart to have a close relationship with the one who embodies perfection?

From beginning to end the Bible is the story of how that way has been made. Every page tells us that our failure is not final. Proverbs 24:16 says, *"A righteous man may fall seven times, but he gets up again."* Even the best people will stumble at times. Even people who are trying their best to do what's right, sometimes get it wrong. Successful people are not people who never fail! I'd rather have someone work for me who tried heroically and failed spectacularly than a mediocre play-safe.

The apostle Paul is a great example of this. He wrote, *"We are hard pressed on every side, but not crushed. Perplexed but not in despair ... struck down but not destroyed"* (2 Corinthians 4:8-9). In other words, you've not failed until you throw in the towel – until you give up.

The 1981 film *Chariots of Fire* told the true story of Scottish athlete Eric Liddell, known as the Flying Scotsman, who went on to become a missionary in China. He refused to run on a Sunday, so in the Olympics he had to withdraw from the 100 meter race, his best event. Instead, he entered the 400 meters. As he went to the starting blocks, an American masseur slipped a piece of paper into Liddell's hand with a quotation from 1 Samuel 2:30: *"Those who honor me I will honor."* Liddell ran with that piece of paper in his hand and not only won the race, but broke the world record.

But another scene earlier in the film inspires me most. Liddell ran in an event between England, Ireland and Scotland. When the gun sounded there was a lot of shoving for the inside lane. He collided with J. J. Gillies of England, and fell. He sat dazed for a moment, not knowing whether he could get up. An official screamed, "Get up and run!"

Liddell jumped to his feet and in his unorthodox style took off after the pack, which was about twenty yards ahead of him. Over a quarter of a mile race that's a big distance to make up. With forty yards to go, he was back in third place, then second. Right at the tape he pulled his head back, passed Gillies, stuck his chest out, won, and then collapsed in total exhaustion. Medics had to carry him off the track.

An article appeared the next day in *The Scotsman*. "The circumstances in which Liddell won the race made it a performance bordering on the miraculous. Veterans whose memories take them back more than thirty-five years in the history of athletics were unanimous in the opinion that Liddell's win was the greatest track performance they had ever seen." Why was it so great? Because there's something glorious about getting up after you've been knocked down. If you don't stay down, you're a winner.

Everybody stumbles in the race of life. Failure is going to be a part of the rest of your life. It's normal, part of being human. The Bible says, *"All have sinned and fall short of the glory of God ..."* Now, of course, not all failure is a result of sin, but the Greek word for sin used here literally means "missed the mark so as not to gain the prize". I once heard about a pastor preaching on this verse, "All have fallen short ..." who said, "Thank God, he forgives our falling shorts!" It's true! We all have falling shorts or short fallings!

Recently, in the small group I am part of we've begun to talk about our "lifelines". Mapping out our lives, we have put on paper the ups and downs of our own stories to tell one another. It's incredible how that kind of honesty can bond people together: when we're real about the ups and downs.

If ever there was a man with ups and downs it was Simon Peter. One of the most "successful failures" in the Bible, my heart warms to him as I read about him. I'm sure many of you will resonate with his life story too.

Peter is the guy who ends up in lots of old jokes as the guy holding the keys to the gates of heaven when people get there (a pretty important job!) But an amazing journey of ups and downs took him to that elevated mythological position – a true story of success and failure – since he was a man who was always jumping in with both feet and getting himself into trouble.

Ups and downs diagram

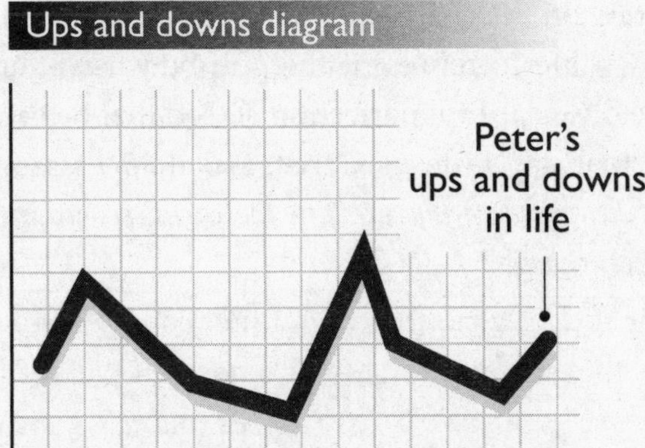

UP

What we know about Peter's life starts when Jesus came to him and said, *"Follow me!"* (Luke 5:1-8). He was called from his fishing business to be the lead disciple, first among equals of the initial band of followers – a small group of other young men – and head of the twelve that Jesus designated apostles. Rabbi Jesus changed his name and his life, determined to draw out the potential that was in him as a leader. From that moment on Peter would be the first follower.

DOWN

Peter had a pattern of thinking that was characterized by the phrase, "I know best". He let Jesus into his boat but moaned when given fishing advice from this landlubber carpenter. Eventually, when he did as he was told, he ended up getting a miraculous overflowing catch as a result. His reaction? *"Go away from me Lord, I'm a sinful man!"* (Luke 5:8) This was actually a very appropriate response! How can an imperfect, sinful man relate to God?

I can't draw on the chart a line high enough above Peter's up and down life to represent the gulf between it and the consistent, holy, beautiful perfection of God that he caught of glimpse of that day in Jesus Christ. Isaiah 55:9 simply tells us, *"As the heavens are higher than the earth, so are my ways higher than your ways."*

UP

Like Jesus, Peter walked on water (Matthew 14: 25-31). He was lead disciple so it was his job to follow first. Against all natural danger signals this ordinary man stepped out to do the impossible. Do you know what? He did it! I don't know how many steps he took, but he actually walked on water, like Jesus. What an "up" that must have been!

DOWN

Peter got very wet that day, however, because he took his eyes off Jesus and gave way to fear. He didn't follow perfectly. He was impetuous. He was often over-confident. So what looked like great success for a couple of steps ended up with Jesus having to pull him out. It's a great picture of what happened in his life again and again! He'd be sunk without Jesus.

UP

Peter was not only first to step out, he was the first to see and say who Jesus was! (Matthew 16:15-17). Jesus knew people had been debating who he really was, so he asked his disciples, "Who do you say that I am?" It was Peter who spoke up, "I say you are the Christ, the Son of the living God." Jesus commended him for that insight and said that God the Father had revealed it to him. Jesus told him that knowing this – who Jesus really is – was the key of the kingdom.

Knowing and declaring who Jesus really is, whatever anyone else says, opens the gates of heaven. Knowing Jesus, the anointed Son of God, makes the difference to any imperfect person – anyone who ever got it wrong, whose failures, mistakes and sins should exclude them from God because they fall so short of his glory. Peter was the first to see and say who Jesus is, and Jesus said that he was holding the keys to open up heaven. How good must that have felt?!

DOWN

Read on just a couple of verses though. Peter opens his mouth and puts his foot in it, presuming to tell Jesus what he should and shouldn't do, and ends up being likened to Satan as a result because he is trying to put a stumbling block in the way of God's plans. The Son of God saying you're collaborating with the enemy? That's a big failure!

UP

It's the last supper. In Matthew 26:33 Peter has a rush of blood and promises to stick with Jesus to the end no matter what.

DOWN

That was a fail! Just as Jesus predicted ahead of time, the rooster crowed when Peter chickened out. His failure could be classed as one of the worst betrayals by Jesus' friends as he denies Jesus three times to save his own skin. Standing by a fire the *coal man* said he didn't know him. He even swore. "Look, I don't *+%$!^ know him!" It doesn't get much lower than this.

UP

But the cross was not the end of Jesus' story or Peter's! After Jesus was resurrected he personally appeared to hundreds of his disciples – ate with them, even cooked for them. He kept saying he wanted to meet particularly with Peter. He had a message and a meeting with Peter in mind. Why? John 20:15 shows us how the one who had denied Jesus three times was the first person to be publicly reinstated. On a beach, after Peter has failed at the only other thing he knows how to do, fishing, and standing by another fire, three times Jesus asked him, "Do you love me?" Do you know how that conversation ended? What words were spoken at the end of that meeting? The very same words it all started with years before: "Follow me!" It's as if, in Jesus' eyes, none of the stuff that happened in between mattered. Jesus had never been surprised by Peter's failures, he had predicted it and already forgiven it. But had Peter learned from it? Maybe the ups and downs were over?

UP

After Jesus' ascension to heaven, Peter, who had been a chicken when Jesus was crucified, stands up in the same city where it happened, Jerusalem, and preached a lion-heart sermon. Three thousand people responded and became Christians!

DOWN

In that sermon (Acts 2:17) he quoted a passage in the Old Testament that promised that the Holy Spirit would now be poured out on all flesh – all people. But contrary to Jesus' final instructions to go into the entire world and preach to the people of all nations, Peter goes nowhere. He doesn't leave Jerusalem. He certainly doesn't go to the Gentiles, to non-Jewish people.

UP

It takes a dramatic vision where Jesus makes all food and all people Kosher, explaining that non-Jewish people can be acceptable to God too, to get Peter to cross the doorstep of a Gentile soldier and tell him about Jesus' life, death, resurrection and message. How many times does he have the vision, each time saying a big fat "No" to it? Three times! (Can you see there's a pattern here!). Peter gets it eventually and becomes the first apostle to reach out to non-Jewish people in Cornelius' house, where the whole family become Christians.

DOWN

In Acts chapter 15 Peter says he knows God chose him to be the one to reach out to Gentiles, but it ends up being the apostle Paul and not Peter who becomes the apostle to the Gentiles. One day Paul even had to publicly chew Peter out about his continued racial double standards in which he continually says non-Jews are acceptable to God, but is not being willing to spend time with them.

So, if you get to the gates of heaven and Peter is there holding the keys like in the cartoons, and you're standing next to an Irishman, a Scotsman and a Jew, you might want to ask him: how do imperfect people get in? How do imperfect, up-and-down people relate to a God who is absolutely consistent, who is holy, holy, holy? How do we get in the gates of heaven Peter? How do people who fail, who have failed, who will fail again – earthly creatures so up and down and far away even during the "ups" from God's perfect standards – how can we connect intimately now and forever to an awesome, majestic, perfect God? How can failures be saved? How can you and I be "perfect failures"?

THE GRACE PLAN

Acts 15 describes the time when Barnabas and Paul were preaching in a place called Antioch - a place where predominately non-Jewish people were becoming Christians. Then a group of Christian followers of Jesus from a Jewish background turned up and began to teach the men there that if they wanted to be real Christians, they had to be circumcised; they had to follow the customs of Moses, obey the dietary laws and so on. In other words they had to behave like Jews in order to be acceptable to God.

You may know that throughout the Old Testament there are signs of our perfect God's promise to bless and do good to imperfect people. To Noah, the sign that accompanied the promise was a rainbow. Later God appeared to a very old, childless Iraqi called Abraham and said, "If you follow me, I'll bless you and your millions of descendants." They entered into a covenant, and as a sign of that promise a sacrifice was made. Then later, the Law was given to Moses and God said, "If you keep all these commandments perfectly, I will be with you and bless you." The sign of that agreement was circumcision (I'm sure Moses would have preferred a rainbow). Circumcision was a sign that the Jews were taking the Law on board as the way of attempting to connect with God – to be saved by keeping his Law.

So these men from a Jewish background talked over Paul and Barnabas' sermons and got alongside the new, non-Jewish Christ-followers, saying that the plan of salvation was to follow Jesus, who was a Jew, and who was himself circumcised. They said, you can't be saved otherwise. God is going to check your pants. They insisted, you have to follow Jesus AND live like a Jew, eat like a Jew, and follow all the customs and commands of Jewish people. You must follow Jesus AND follow the Law as perfectly as possible. So as an outward sign that you are going to live according to the Law, you must be circumcised. Otherwise, you're not saved; you're not really a Christian.

The problem was: these guys were not born Jewish. The Bible tells us that Paul and Barnabas ended up having a sharp debate with the other Jewish Christians over the issue. You can translate that as a big row! They say, "No! These guys don't need to be circumcised. There is no 'Jesus plus the Law' plan. There is only the 'Jesus plan'!" They didn't manage to successfully resolve the argument, however, so they decided: "Let's get this settled once and for all. We'll go to the guys who first knew Jesus and walked with him in Galilee and get an opinion. We'll talk to the apostles back in Jerusalem."

So they meet together with the apostles and church leaders and tell them how everywhere the gospel is spoken, people who are not Jews are believing it. So what do we do?

The Bible tells us that some of the Christians in the church were Pharisees – a legalistic faction who strictly observed the Law. They agreed with the other teachers who said this new group of believers ought to be circumcised and follow the "Jesus plus the Law" plan. They should follow Jesus and try to be perfect, they said.

But it is at this point in the discussion that a perfect failure stands up to speak. Remember, Peter had been brought up as a Law-observing Jew. He'd been circumcised. Now he wants to answer this question once and for – the biggest and most important question ever, in fact, because the eternal well-being of multitudes of lives hang in the balance. You can sense the frustration in his words. He knows better than anyone that we have all failed and we will all fail again. Reflecting on the ups and downs of his life, Peter sees that the only one who has been consistent and perfect in his story is Jesus, from the day he first heard him call, "Follow me!" Here is what he says about how we can be saved (Acts 15:7-11):

> *"You know that some time ago God made a choice among you that the Gentiles might hear from my lips the message of the gospel and believe. God, who knows the heart, showed that he accepted them by giving the Holy Spirit to them, just as he did to us. He made no distinction between us and them, for he purified their hearts by faith. Now then, why do you try to test God by putting on the necks of the disciples a yoke that neither we nor our fathers have been able to bear? No! We believe it is through the grace of our Lord Jesus that we are saved, just as they are."*

Looking closer at what Peter tells them, this is amazing! He is saying, "It doesn't matter where these guys are from or what their background is. All that matters is, we preached to them about Jesus and they believed! That changes everything."

God knows our hearts. Even if we manage to fool people outwardly, put on a good show, God knows what we're like on the inside. BUT, because of Jesus, because of God's grace, he accepts us and will make us acceptable.

God gives us his Holy Spirit. He comes to live in us by his presence. He doesn't come to live in people who are perfect or those who have been trying really hard to be good. He doesn't come to live in those who have undergone some kind of religious ceremony or who've been circumcised "outwardly". He comes to live inside those whose hearts have been changed – those who have invited him to come and make a difference in their life. The Bible says that God purifies imperfect hearts like that. How? By faith. How can we have a pure heart before God when we know we've thought, said and done wrong things? We have to have our heart purified by him.

Listen again to the conclusion Peter reaches: "Why do you want to keep trying to live in a way that we know has never worked? We are never going to live UP to that. We can't live up to God's standards of perfection. We need his grace to come down to us."

The "be perfect by keeping the Law and commands perfectly" plan doesn't work. It didn't work for imperfect people like us then and it won't work now. God's Law and his commandments don't show us how to be saved – they just tell us that we need to be! We can't save ourselves. There is no "Jesus and ...", no "Jesus plus something else". There is only Jesus. That's the grace plan. Look at the illustration below. Grace is God's perfect antidote to our imperfections and failures. The grace of Jesus is what God has said can make failures perfect. He says, "Follow me" and from the day we say yes to that, we connect by grace to his perfection.

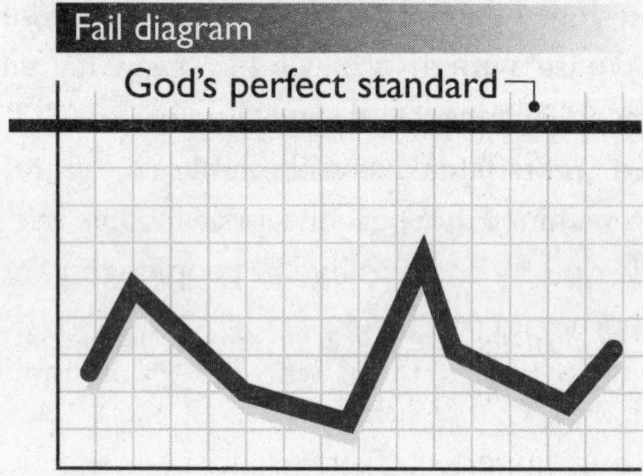

So it's Jesus or nothing for us, because Jesus was the only perfect man who ever lived. He is the only sinless person – the only one qualified to save us – and He did it all for us on the cross. If we handed in the test paper of our lives in the perfection examination we'd get a FAIL! But someone else took the test for us. His perfect obedience, sacrifice on the cross, and resurrection means that Jesus got an A*, 100%, absolute perfection. And now, whenever we need it most, He says to us, "You can have my result instead of yours." (This is the offer God extends to every one of us today. Have you accepted it?)

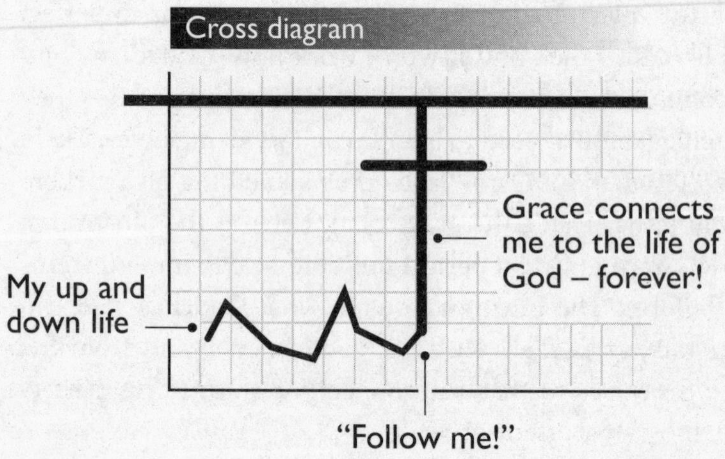

What a difference it makes to live knowing we've already achieved a pass with flying colors! How do failing and imperfect people connect and stay connected to God? It's not complicated. Years later, Peter, the *perfected* failure, wrote a letter and explained how it all works in one line (1 Peter 3:18):

> *"For Christ died for sins once for all, the righteous for the unrighteous, to bring you to God."*

We trade our imperfection for Christ's perfection! Look again at the diagram and you'll see what I mean.

The only absolutely consistent love, faithfulness and perfection in Peter's life was Jesus. Jesus said, "Follow me" and the two of them connected. Once that has happened, nothing can separate us from the love of God that is in Christ Jesus! Whenever Peter failed, Jesus pulled him up, pulled him out and brought him back.

Whenever, however, wherever we blow it, Jesus wants us back! He comes looking for us, not to punish us, but because we matter to Him and because He has a job, a purpose for us. No matter how badly you feel you have blown it. No matter how deep the hole you have dug for yourself. Jesus comes looking to restore you and give you a reason not just to exist, but to live! He walks right into the heartbreak of our hard-working but fruitless hours, and invites us to try again, His way, in His power.

It's not, "Never fail and then you can follow me," it's just, "Follow me! With all your ups and downs." Like a teacher at the beginning of term who says, "You've already got an A, so now that pressure is off let's really have some fun and start learning together" I can try and fail and pick up and start again because I'm on the grace plan. I've already got an A! The most important A ever: ACCEPTANCE. Acceptance from God. He sees my failures, but more importantly he sees me as perfected by grace. If you accept his grace today, then he will accept you forever.

We who have failed in the past and will fail again connect to Jesus' perfection by *grace.* Peter, who knew he had failed in the past, fails now, and will fail in the future, came to know that he had been saved, was being saved, and would be saved in the future – all because he had been accepted and perfected by grace, a free gift of God's love through Jesus. This is how we, or anyone, are saved.

So what do Christ's followers believe? That we're perfect? No. We fail. Do we believe we are better than anyone else? No way, quite the opposite. But, to paraphrase Chumbawama, "We get knocked down, but we get up again."

Because of the cross we can live as perfected failures. And to do that is not failure, but success.

Father
Fitness
Friends
JESUS
Finances
Family
Failures

"All I ask is the chance to prove that money can't make me happy."

—Spike Milligan

FOUR

Finance

[balancing act]

I was nineteen. It was a hot day at the training school. I'd been doing hard physical exercise all day and had a big lunch. Then we had a boring talk lined up, someone from the Police's pensions and finance department with a degree in total monotony, coming to tell us about money. A practical session about avoiding debt … living within your means … spending and investing wisely …. blah, blah, blah … I lasted about ten minutes. I thought I'd close my eyes, just for a few moments.

I got away with it. I just looked like I was thinking, hard. Wow, it's stuffy in this room. Drone .... drone ... pensions ... savings ... taxes ... drone … Just a few more seconds with my eyes closed, then I'll nod and look like I'm thinking really hard.

What seemed like two seconds later, I was prodded by John, the copper next to me. He was smiling widely. I smiled back. Until I saw the face of the boss who was giving the talk. Not impressed. Glaring.

Why? Surely it was only a matter of moments? Then I felt the large damp patch on the front of my shirt. It turns out I'd been gone about twenty minutes. Fully gone. Loudly snoring, sniffing and (yes) slobbering. Head rolling back and forward and from side-to-side like Homer Simpson in church. It's safe to say, as I look back, the subject of money and finances didn't interest me much.

This was the Eighties, the decade of decadence. It cost big money to really dress like a fool back then. Around the same time I began to earn pretty good money. I went into a cool men's clothes shop where I ogled the baggy shirts and twelve pleat Bowie trousers I craved. I was greeted by a mulleted bloke who looked like an extra from Miami Vice. A few years above me at my old school, this guy now worked here and really looked the part (as I reflect on it now I won't tell you which part).

This bloke was always way too cool at school and had never even spoke to me. Suddenly, now he took a very keen interest in showing me the latest styles, many of which really suited me (he said). I had only gone in for a leather tie, but he showed me a nice two tone suit with the smallest lapels imaginable and some great shoes to go with it. I was getting worried about not being able to afford it until he kindly offered me a store card so I could take it away, get a discount on what I'd bought and then make "easy payments" on it. Bargain! I rolled the sleeves up and wore it all weekend in the clubs. But I paid for it for years.

In fact, it wasn't until I got married that someone far more sensible than me said she was going to cut up that card and pay it all off – ouch! – not just make minimum payments on the interest. I slowly realized that the shopkeepers and sales people were not really my friends at all. They didn't really want to help me. They were not in business to save me money. They wanted to relieve me of my hard-earned cash to give themselves a nice fat bonus. It's all too easy these days to become unbalanced in the area of our finances, and I have to watch myself very closely even now, to stop that happening.

> "We needed something to worship and something to believe in and have long since swapped God with Gucci. We have been living beyond our means, in debt beyond our ability to pay, in the naive but hopeful belief that this would be the bubble that would never burst."
> —Neil Lawson, All Consuming

BALANCING ACT

Some of you know you really need to read this chapter on finances, but you don't want to. As J John says, "Just when you started to make ends meet, somebody moved the ends!" You're not balancing the books. Maybe you are one of those guys who can't help acting on impulse, so you buy stuff you don't need to impress people you don't like with money you don't have. You think saving money means you bought something in a sale. Read on my friend. I've been there and I hope to help.

There are others who will be tempted to skim this section because you're doing okay, relatively speaking (while you think a little extra income wouldn't hurt, even J. D. Rockefeller, when he was asked how much money it would take to make him happy, said, "Just a little bit more.") Please bear with me, because even though you've got money in the bank, you may have something to learn here too.

I remember from physics that when there is balance, there's less friction. I was also taught that being out of balance results in acceleration, until something happens to re-establish equilibrium. The laws of balance apply not just for the tightrope walker, ballet dancer or gymnast, they also apply in the area of our finances. You go to the cash-point and you want to check your what? Your balance. Your business, organization, or the church you lead – all of them need to have their books checked from time to time, to have the auditors make sure everything is in order.

There are certain principles that will help us to balance anything. If we apply these to the area of our finances, we can achieve balance there too – and less friction! If you flout the laws of financial balance and break them, you'll end up broke. This will happen whether you are an individual, a business, a bank or even a nation. Things can accelerate out of control very quickly. If you want to achieve balance, you need to remember and apply the three A's: *aim*, *attention* and *adjustment*.

> "Your yearnings will always exceed your earnings."
> —J John

Before I get into that, a word for anyone with major debt issues. Have you ever tried to balance on one leg? It's harder than it looks. Now get someone to put just one finger on your elbow to support you and it's easier. If you're seriously out of balance then you need support. Just having someone come to stand alongside you really makes a difference psychologically. You're not alone.

The last thing you want is one of these loan shark companies on the TV that masquerade as solutions but just land you in more debt. I highly recommend you contact with a charitable organization like CAP (Christians Against Poverty) who have helped many thousands by giving genuinely free support and advice which can get you headed toward a debt-free future. That's an achievable aim for you, right now.

AIM

If a gymnast sets out to make their way across a narrow beam, they don't look down at their feet. They focus on a fixed point in the distance. Someone stretching in the gym in a Pilates class gets told when balancing to "Aim at a spot on the wall." You have to have an aim to be in balance. A good financial adviser would ask you what your aim for your money is.

Some people aim to just make all they can. You can quickly end up way off balance like that. Some of us guys use this as a barometer of self-worth – we can all too easily equate what we own or earn with how much we're worth. But if continued accumulation drives your life, you will never be satisfied and you will inevitably have relational issues. The Bible never says money is evil, it's just a commodity of exchange that can be used for good or ill. What is does says is that, *"The **love** of money is the root of all kinds of evil"* (1 Timothy 6:10). You may have the Midas touch, but you know how his story ended! It's madness to think that more money equates to more happiness. How many times do we hear about lottery winners who end up blowing it all big time?

Some men will answer, "Well, I just aim to provide for my loved ones." Noble words. But often misguided. Savoo.co.uk recently commissioned a survey of 2,500 British working dads to study their attitudes towards family life. When asked to identify the roles they perceived as their key responsibilities within their own family unit, three quarters of those questioned identified themselves more as a bread-winner than they did a father. In the same survey, three quarters said they wished they spent less time working and more time with their kids.

Providing for your loved ones is a great thing to do, in fact the Bible commands it as a proof that we really know God. 1 Timothy 5:8 in the Message version puts it very strongly: *"Anyone who neglects to care for family members in need repudiates the faith."* But we've all met people who were good at looking after their family financially but not relationally. Kids want our presence more than our presents! Additionally, people may be very generous to their friends and themselves, but that doesn't always mean they are able to be generous towards the things of God. "Charity begins at home," but it has to make it out the door first. Aiming to provide for your loved ones alone won't lead to true financial balance.

Your aim may be to *save* a lot of money. That can be commendable too, but as Jesus' parable of the rich fool reminds us in Luke 12, one day you will be pushing up the daisies instead of piling up the interest, and who'll get it all then? Saving is very important, but it's not the be all and end all of your finances. You may not be very much fun to live with if all you want to do with your money is save it! You could be someone who could stand up and give lectures about how to invest money and own stocks and shares galore, but that doesn't mean you are financially balanced. True financial wisdom doesn't just extend ten or twenty years into the future – it takes account of eternal realities.

Maybe your aim is simply to "Spend, spend, spend!" It may not be your *stated* aim, but objectively observing your life, it's how you live. People in our society have moved on from keeping up with the Joneses to trying to catch up with the Beckhams – like the ads promised we all could. In a global recession it's easy to point the finger at greedy bankers, ineffective regulators and bent politicians, but in the end, we spent the money! We wanted stuff so we bought it, we defined ourselves by it, we shopped till the economy dropped.

AIM FOR FREEDOM

Can I suggest a great aim for your finances? To be financially free. What do I mean by financial freedom? The picture most would have of financial freedom is to have no money worries at all, so we can do whatever we want. That sounds like a good aim, but I'd say it's only half way there.

We all know stories of people who have multiple millions and yet their lives end up a complete wreck. We hear about people who certainly had enough money, but everything went down the pan. As the writer Helen Gurley Brown put it, "Money, if it does not bring you happiness, will at least help you be miserable in comfort."

You probably think that if you had that kind of money you'd be clever enough not to waste it? Well one insurance company calculated that on average, every person in Britain will spend £1.5 million during their lifetime. You can make all you can, splurge all you can, save all you can, look after your family ... all well and good. But good enough?

How about this as an aim? To not have to worry about money, because you simply have enough to do whatever God wants? That was the way Jesus Christ lived during his time on the earth and he said we can live like that too. He made it the centerpiece of his financial advice:

> *"Your heavenly Father knows that you need all these things. But seek first his kingdom and his righteousness, and all these things will be added to you. So do not worry about tomorrow; for tomorrow will care of itself."* (Matthew 6:32-33)

AIM TO HONOR

Whether thinking about saving, spending, investing or giving, the Bible is consistent in its message: if you want true financial balance, your aim should be to *seek kingdom things first*. What does that mean exactly? It means to honor God with everything. Why? Well, this may sound weird to some of you, but I believe that "giving back" is a fundamental principle of life.

There is a phrase that is used in one of the Church of England prayer books that reminds worshippers of this aim. It comes right out of some words in the Old Testament, spoken by one of the richest and wisest men who ever lived, king David, on a day when he gave away literally tons of his own gold to fund building work on the temple in Jerusalem. He said these beautiful words that sum up his attitude with regard to wealth and how he aimed to use it:

> Yours, Lord, is the greatness, the power, the glory, the splendor, and the majesty; for everything in heaven and on earth is yours. All things come from you, and of your own do we give you.

God gave everything to you in the first place. As these words say, *all* good things come from him. So anything we give back to him or to others is a natural and grateful response to his generosity and love.

Disraeli said of a boasting MP called John Bright, who had declared himself a "self-made man": "Yes, and he is very much in love with his creator." However much we make, we are not self-made at all. Anyone who has ever been able to do anything, whatever the achievement, owes that accomplishment to the God who enabled it. That's what king David realized as he looked at all his "stuff".

Even though from a human perspective David had led well, fought hard, and made some courageous decisions and sacrifices to amass the wealth, position and prestige he enjoyed, he was humble enough not to take the credit for it. He knew God was at work – in an upfront way as well as behind the scenes – to give him "all things". So, this earthly king made a decision to seek God's kingdom first. He aimed at being faithful in looking after everything with which he was entrusted.

AIM TO TITHE

Everything changes when we get that same perspective. I know that I have been given a lot to look after, but I am not really the owner of it. Everything I have is on loan to me, for the short amount of time I am on earth. People who have this perspective have a different aim with their money, time and talents. They say, "All things come from you, God." Their aim is to please him with all of it. That's where I believe true financial freedom starts – as we no longer worry, but do what God says with all he gives us.

Years ago, as a new Christian, I was taught about tithing. To tithe literally means to give a tenth back to God. Simply, the rule of thumb is that God gives you 100% and you give him 10% back. The Bible teaches that God's people historically gave back at least that amount (actually a number of tenths) to the poor, for community celebration and for worship. It's not hard to calculate. If you receive £10 you give him £1 back. £10,000? Do the math. As a minister, that's the principle I've taught for years in every church and it's the way I have always worked personally – living on 90% of my earnings to give 10% back to my local church and then after that to be generous with the rest of the money.

I know a lot of you are a long way off from thinking like that! I know for some people this seems out of reach. But don't tune me out at this point. Please keep on reading.

Firstly, I want you to understand something: God doesn't need your money. He doesn't want anything *from* you, but He wants something *for* you: to grow in trust and dependence on him, which looks a lot like what the Bible would call faith. Tithing is a sign that God is in charge of your life, that he rules you – not greed or need or want. In my own life tithing has been like the stabilizers on a bike. It brings balance. It broke something of the power of materialism and got me started on living as a financially free person – free to be generous.

Tithing is a biblical principle, not a mechanism designed to twist God's arm and squeeze blessing out of him. It is not correct to see it as some sort of transaction whereby, "I have given God his 10%. He's got his cut, so now I get to do whatever I want to do with the 90%." Nothing in the Bible would support that kind of thinking. We are not supposed to just honor God with a fraction of our money, but with EVERYTHING! That should be our aim.

Imagine I have a caravan. Actually I do have one. Imagine a beautiful one in the Lake District. That's mine again. Imagine you ask me to use it for a holiday for a week and I agree (it probably wouldn't happen, but we're imagining aren't we?) What percentage of the caravan do you think I'd want you to look after? Would I be happy if I found it full of empty takeaway wrappings, smelling like a lay-by burger van, dented and scratched, but you were able to point out to me the shiny, clean wheel trims? No way! It doesn't work like that does it? (Wow! This scenario is much too scary for me to imagine. I know my wife and how much she loves that caravan!) You'd be expected to look after the whole of it, not just a part.

What should be our aim financially? God is looking for us to honor him with all of our money, not just a percentage. God says, "I expect you to manage everything I have given you in a way that honors me." With regards to my income, expenditure, saving, giving and pensions, the filter question should always be: "God, how do I honor you?" Which leads us to the next practical thing we have to do to balance our financial affairs.

ATTENTION

If you're going to honor God with all he gave you, what matters most is not your pay, but that you *pay attention*. I went to a circus skills event for kids recently and couldn't help having a go at everything myself. The stern looking clown gave me one of those plates to spin on a stick. "Rule number one? Keep your eye on it! Look where it is going, or it'll come down with a crash! Pay attention!"

When it comes to money, we often focus on the wrong thing: how much we have – our income. That is key, of course. But we actually need to look more at what is going *out*. Financial balance is a lot to do with simply paying attention. You can't balance anything with your eyes shut, whether it's spinning a plate, standing on stilts, or a budget. If you don't know where it's going, you'll wonder where it went.

In Bible times a lot of money could be made from wool, so the more sheep you owned, the richer you were. Proverbs 27:23 says, *"Be sure you know the condition of your flocks, give careful attention to your herds."* Perhaps you are familiar with the saying, "Keep an eye on the pennies and the pounds will look after themselves." Can I encourage you for the next week or so, before trying to do anything differently with your money, as you think about a different aim, to simply pay ATTENTION to your income and expenditure. Notice what you spend money on this week – even the little things. Write down everything you spend for a week. Make a note somewhere and review it at the end of the week.

Ignorance is NOT bliss! So often I've spoken with people who don't want to open their bank statements or credit card bills. But it's not a happy financial state that is stopping them from doing so. It is pure terror! If you don't keep track you'll get off track. I'm inviting you to act like a financial planner – the Bible would use the word "steward" – to track where your money is going. In its simplest form, budgeting is a written note of how much is coming in, how much is going out, and noticing the difference.

For some people, a budget is just a confirmation of their worst nightmare. But it's only when you know where your money is actually going that you can hope to budget for where you want it to go in the future. Could you do that for this coming week? Whether you're using cash, cards or cheques, keep track of where your money is going for one week.

It may help you to draw out the cash you think you will need and use that instead of cards. I know that's counter-cultural these days. Banks and retailers have combined to try to make us feel that cash is somehow old hat. Why is that? Well, I've noticed something about spending: Cash hurts, plastic doesn't. If I go into a shop and have to pay cash, I don't get that money back and I certainly walk out of there with less of it. But if I pay by card, I get the card handed back to me and it looks just the same – it doesn't even shrink! That's the lure of plastic. The lie is that is it's not costing you anything, at least, not yet.

Notice what your money is going on month by month. If you make decisions that commit all your income to servicing debts or a lifestyle you can't afford because you won't "act your wage", you'll find it practically impossible to be generous when others have a need or you feel you should support a God-honoring vision. Even if your heart is moved to give, your purse won't stretch. It's already gone, or going, elsewhere. It's now a sofa, a car or a TV. If you've spent it, you can't give it or save it now. I know that's obvious, but so often we act like it's not. Decisions can tie you up, or set you free. And whenever a person makes decisions that result in them living out of balance financially, they also end up out of balance in their relationship with God.

Two thousand ago, Jesus Christ said some incredibly insightful things about money that are still every bit as appropriate to people in our day.

> "For where your treasure is there your heart will be also." (Matthew 6:21)

What is your treasure? It's revealed by whatever you spend most of your money on. And wherever a person's treasure is, Jesus says, that's where their heart is going to be. If our heart is in a particular company, we'll buy shares in it. If our heart is in a particular football team, we'll buy a season ticket. Our financial aims and where we invest our money will make apparent what matters most to us.

That's why Jesus talked way more about money than he did heaven and hell. In fact, if I, as a minister, were to place the same emphasis on talking about money as Jesus did, I'd have to preach about it every month.

To assess somebody's spirituality, don't look at whether or not they are in church on Sunday, how loud they sing or whether they say long prayers. God is not fooled by that. If you really want to know where someone's heart is in relation to God, you need to look at their bank statement. It's a litmus test. Your heart is where your money goes. What Jesus said is true of all of us. He notices. He sat in the temple and observed what people put in the offering. He paid attention not to the amount, but to the *proportion* of income people gave. We should too.

Jesus went on to say,

> *"No one can serve two masters. Either he will hate the one and love the other, or he will be devoted to the one and despise the other. You cannot serve both God and Money."* (Matthew 6:24)

The word "money" in this verse comes from an Aramaic word, *mammon,* which was also the name given to the false god of wealth. As you begin to look how you're spending your money, you'll also become aware of *who* you are really living for. The truth is, there is a battle for your heart being waged every day. This is a tension that will never go away while we're here on this earth. Are you going to be possessed by your possessions? Avarice, accumulation and acquisition – will your security and hope be in that? Will you just want God to serve you by helping you in that pursuit, or will you serve God and surrender everything? You can't have it both ways.

ADJUSTMENT

If you want to keep anything balanced, you need to have an *aim,* pay *attention* to it, and finally make necessary *adjustments* (big or small).

I'm not going to presume to tell you what adjustments you need to make, but let me establish a principle. Some preachers make it sound as though *all* God wants is your money. But God is after the real treasure of your heart. Your heavenly Father invites you to surrender your finances back to him, the one who gave it to you in the first place. Once you surrender all your "stuff" – your savings, debts, income and expenditure – then he has what he wants: your heart, and you will worry a lot less about what you want, because now he's in charge of that.

Recently, after I spoke about this issue in my church, Dan wrote to me to say he had decided not to spend so much on a TV sports subscription that would only have taken time away from his wife and kids anyway. He had decided he was going to give away the money he'd saved. Fantastic! I wouldn't have told him to do that. There's nothing in the Bible that says, "Thou shalt not spend money on Sky Sports." But he had thought about his aim – the aim of honoring God – paid attention to his spending decisions, thought about the repercussions of those decisions, and made an adjustment.

Paul recently told me he had said no to a promotion at work and the extra money that would bring, because he realised saying "yes" to the extra hours would mean saying "no" a lot more to his family. He judged that the money wasn't worth it. How much is money worth to you?

One man's adjustments may not be the same as the ones you and I need to make. We are all different. Some people have adjusted with regard to their savings or investments or pensions. The Bible is clear that wise people save, while fools don't (see Proverbs 21:20). 28% of Britons don't even have a savings account. Maybe you'd be wise to make an adjustment in that area?

Or perhaps you need to adjust your view of debt. A couple of decades ago being in debt was frowned upon as evidence that someone was not in control of their finances. But within the last few years there has been a real cultural shift towards debt becoming the norm for most families. The best adjustment I could ever advise you to make regarding debt is to avoid it and get out of it as soon as possible without taking on any more. Proverbs 22:7 says (even if you don't believe the Bible is the word of God, you've got to know this is true), *"The borrower is servant to the lender."* You can translate "servant" as "slave". There's a reason they call it "Mastercard"!

If you don't think the lender is really master, try defaulting on a loan and see what happens. What does being a slave mean? It means I don't get to do what I want to do, I have to do something else. Debt means you can't give like you want to, live like you want to, save like you want to. We end up consuming our way, one purchase at a time, into a place where we have no freedom. Some of you are going to make that adjustment even today. You are reading this and deciding to draw a line in the sand, making a decision towards freedom and generosity – for less stress and greed, less spending, more saving and an attitude of gratitude.

Our culture makes us feel like we never have enough. Edmund Burke wrote in 1757, "The great error of our nature is not to know where to stop; not to be satisfied with any reasonable acquirement ... but to lose all we have gained by an insatiable pursuit of more." We forget how fortunate we are. We have enough and some to spare, yet still we hanker for more.

If you've ever traveled around the world to anywhere approaching the poverty line, not just on a package holiday where they shield you from it, but up close with the reality, then you may be aware of how fortunate you are. If you're living indoors, have food on the table and a change of clothes to wear, then you belong to a small but massively privileged minority that exists in the world. In the West we throw away, on average, 2kgs of uneaten food every day. We give our leftovers to our pets and have to carry our fat dogs to the vets whilst 15 million children worldwide die of malnutrition every year.

Go to www.globalrichlist.com and put in how much income you have been given. The office of National Statistics says the average UK worker earns £23,400. You may earn substantially more or less, but the average person in developing countries is living on less than £1.70 a day – not even £600 a year! Do you have a car? If the world were a village of 1,000 people, only 70 people would own a car. Do you own a computer? Only 4% of people in the world own one. You are a blessed person! You've already won the lottery!

Here's a suggested adjustment. What I want you to do is to look back over the last year and work out the total amount of money you gave away to charity (the Church, the poor or whatever). Now work out what percentage of your income – of all that God entrusted to you – that equates to. Most of us think we're more generous then we actually are. J John says, "When it comes to giving, most people stop at nothing." The average Briton gives away 0.8% of their income to charity. Less than 1%! Hopefully, you're ahead of that.

Challenge yourself today: make your financial *aim* to give God first place in your finances, rather than more "stuff". Pay *attention* to the reality, not only of your personal world, but the bigger picture God is concerned with. Then make the necessary *adjustments* you need to make to be financially balanced – free to honor him with your money and able to do what he wants with everything he's entrusted to you.

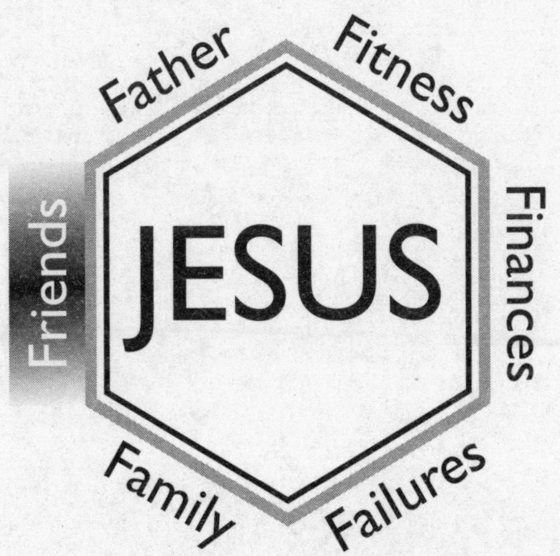
Father
Fitness
Friends
JESUS
Finances
Family
Failures

"The bird a nest, the spider a web, man friendship."

—William Blake

FIVE

Friends

[who's your best friend?]

At primary school I had a best friend. I don't know when Paul became my best friend, but it happened well before he turned to me one day and asked the childish question that either breaks or cements it for sure – that point at which you turn to someone and say, "Who's your best friend?"

Depending on the person's response you can go on to confirm, "Am I your best friend then?" or you can ask, "Will you be my best friend?" Of course, there is always the risk the other person will turn round and say, "No, I don't want to be your best friend." But to hear a "yes" is definitely worth that risk.

From the age of seven through to ten, Paul was my best friend. Even though he was posh. I knew he was posh because his mum and dad had a car. He was smaller than me, with a shock of blonde hair. We laughed all the time. We both publicly rebelled against school dinners together. We were deadly Kung Fu fighters at playtime. And in class we drew superhero cartoons. We knew one day we'd have our own version of DC or Marvel comics.

Six months before the end of primary school, however, Paul told me his parents were moving him away and they were all going to live a long, long way away. (I now realise it wasn't that far, but your world is so much smaller when you're a kid!) My family didn't own a car. We didn't have a phone. He gave me his phone number. Like I said, he was posh. One day I walked to the phone box at the end of the road, dialed a number, and a very posh boy came on the other end of the line. But for some reason I couldn't speak a word to him and just put the receiver down.

That's the sad tale of how I lost my first best friend. You might be heartless enough not to be too moved by it, in which case I don't want *you* to be my friend (I'm kidding), but years later when I was on a counseling course looking at grief, we were given a list of grief symptoms and asked to look back on our lives and think when we first felt grief. The name Paul Marshall surfaced immediately. I also realized that I had spent my high school years looking for a smaller, blonde friend, preferably called Paul, to replace the one I had lost.

Making friends makes you vulnerable.

The offer of friendship and the chance one might be rejected go hand in hand. And friendships change and people come and go. Once you have a friend, they might leave you or you could fall out over something so that they are no longer your friend. Maybe this could spill over from just one individual to a whole group.

Maybe we have been hurt in the past, so we end up isolating ourselves because we have insulated ourselves. A crust forms around our heart. "It's probably better to not put my heart out there again in case I get hurt," we tell ourselves.

BILLY NO-MATES

I just went out for a meal on my ownsome. My wife's at work today. Sometimes I like to do that anyway. The secret is to take a book with you, so you don't look like a loner. You may think this is potty, but sometimes I also carry on a mental conversation with Jesus over a meal like this, because he's promised never to leave me alone. On this occasion, however, even though I had a book to read, I constantly fiddled with my smart-phone and looked busy. I felt like I should somehow justify to the waitress the fact of me not having a friend or significant other with me.

I agree with what God said in the beginning to a man called Adam. Despite him living in the perfect environment with the most fulfilling type of work and having the best boss, God noted: "It's not good for him to be alone."

We're alone too much. Even when we're with people.

Most men haven't got many friends – not really good friends. Women are much better at this than men. One reason for this, I think, is that to be a friend you need to be a good listener and think about the other person's needs, not just your own! Men often do what's called "report speak" – where you just listen for when the other person's sentence finishes so that in the ensuing gap you can say what you want to say. Women tend to be better than men at such "soft" skills, which are actually just good manners. All that stuff about having two ears and only one mouth is true.

> **"I wish I could be a friend like that."**
> (from a talk by Andy Economides)

Proverbs 18:24 says that if you want to have many friends, you have to show yourself to be friendly. How? Friendly people are other-people focused. I love the story from the 19th Century about a woman who had the rare opportunity to dine with the two most famous living Englishmen of her day: Prime Ministers William Gladstone and Benjamin Disraeli. Who impressed her most? She said, "When I went to lunch with William Gladstone I was convinced that I was dining with the greatest living Englishman. But when I went to lunch with Disraeli, I was convinced that he was dining with the greatest living Englishwoman!"

I shudder to think how many times I've missed out on the possibility of making friends because I was too busy making an impression.

In friendships, too often we put up a front. We let people down and they let us down. The temptation is strong to just do superficial relationships instead.

For a long time in my life I was quite happy to just be intimate with my wife and superficial with everyone else. Where did that come from? As a Police Officer I only had mates who were other Police Officers, and some of those relationships, forged in tough circumstances, remain very strong and deep today. A fellow ex-officer who I haven't worked with in decades only yesterday reminded me, "We always stand together." That was true. But I had serious trust issues with other people.

Maybe you can look back on a time in your life when you were part of a band of brothers. But is that still the case today? Superficial is the norm in many workplaces, pubs and churches. Coal men greet each other with, "How's it going?" and a slap on the back, but don't really expect or want an answer. Body language experts tell us the amount of slaps on the back in a man hug increase the more uncomfortable we are and the more quickly we want to get away. For fun, a friend of mine called James has perfected what he calls the "awkward hug", where you don't put your head to either side as one would expect, but keep looking straight ahead and watch what the other, very embarrassed, man does. Only try this with friends!

The only place in our culture where it seems okay for men to show physical affection is on the football pitch after a goal. That's not the case everywhere.

I just got back from a Greek island where I was privileged to visit a very vibrant small church, reaching its community amazingly well (three people were baptized in their mid-week service). At the end, all the Greek men went round and kissed each other on the cheeks. I went to thank the Pastor and he landed a big smacker on me too. To be honest, I'm really rather comfortable with less intimacy than that! But Diamond Geezers aren't afraid to get a bit closer, a bit more real.

My superficiality complex was compounded when I became a Church of England minister and was told, "You can't have friends in the parish." That was the received wisdom of older clergy, plus, a system of moving round the country every few years didn't make for depth of friendship either, because you were always just arriving or getting ready to go. You learned to keep a professional distance. I heard someone say, "You can't lead the people if you need the people." It sounds catchy doesn't it? That became my internal mantra for too long. It leads to a pretty lonely life if you are insulated and isolated.

Now, it's true that one can't be friends with everyone. I have over 800 Facebook friends at today's count – and I'm open to more if you like and don't want to engage me in theological debate – but many of them are people I don't *really* know. British anthropologist Robin Dunbar says the average number of Christmas card contacts we have 150.

Thank God for my wife who does that for us, otherwise nobody would get a card. There's a limit to how many close friends you can have, most sociologists would put it between 6 and 12.

A typical individual's social world might comprise of an inner circle of five "core" people and an additional layer of 10. Some of the people in your central group may be family members. Outside that, there's another 35 in the next circle and another 100 on the outside. How does yours compare? It's easy to get hung up on the numbers and quality matters more than quantity, but who is most important in your life and which relationships are you investing yourself in most in terms of time and energy?

Those of us who are trying to order their lives around what the Bible teaches follow a man who had twelve close mates he lived with 24/7, sharing everything. Three of them were closer than brothers, certainly than his own flesh and blood. He didn't just come to have connection at a distance, but called them his friends (John 15:15). He was intimate and vulnerable. He even washed their feet and was betrayed, with a kiss, by one of them.

I WISH ...

How do we get to a deeper level of friendship? A friend of mine is a missionary, doing incredible work in Nigeria. Someone who believes in his work bought him a car to help his ministry. One day Andy pulled up to preach at a church here in the UK and a little boy was sitting outside in the car park. As he got out of his nice shiny car the boy said, "That's a nice car."

"Oh, my friend gave me this car..." he replied.

The little boy said, "I wish I could be a friend like that."

Notice he didn't say, "I wish I *had* a friend like that."

How often do we think, "How do I get good friends," rather than, "How do I get to be a friend like that?"

I'm further challenged about friendships when I look at the life of one of the central characters of the New Testament, removed from us in time and geography, but a man like us we can learn so much from because of his tremendously rich relational life. This network was forged despite an incredible schedule of travel, during which he endured persecution, problems and prison. Nevertheless, he was incredibly effective in his life mission. But not at the expense of building really close, mutually loving and supportive relationships and friendships.

So the apostle Paul was effective in his mission, but also successful in his relational life. How many men can say that?

Paul must have been on a long journey to arrive at that place, however. The picture I see of him before he was converted is one of a person who didn't have many friends. Why? He hated people – particularly Christians! Yet, when he came to know Jesus Christ on that now famous Damascus road, something changed in his heart because of that primary relationship. And then all his other relationships changed too.

The New Testament preserves for us many of the letters Paul wrote to churches. While they contain teaching, encouragement and the occasional rebuke, often he lists the names of his friends. For example, check out Romans 16. I haven't space to include everyone, but Paul seems to want to make sure nobody gets left out and he has inspiring and encouraging words for all his friends.

> *"Say hello to Priscilla and Aquila, who have worked hand in hand with me in serving Jesus. They once put their lives on the line for me. And I'm not the only one grateful to them. All the non-Jewish gatherings of believers also owe them plenty, to say nothing of the church that meets in their house.*
>
> *Hello to my dear friend Epenetus. He was the very first follower of Jesus in the province of Asia.*
>
> *Hello to Mary. What a worker she has turned out to be!*
>
> *Hello to my cousins Andronicus and Junias. We once shared a jail cell. They were believers in Christ before I was. Both of them are outstanding leaders.*
>
> *Hello to Ampliatus, my good friend in the family of God.*
>
> *Hello to Urbanus, our companion in Christ's work, and my good friend Stachys.*
>
> *Hello to Apelles, a tried-and-true veteran in following Christ ..."*
>
> (Romans 16:3-10, The Message)

The list goes on and one gets the impression that wherever he goes, even though we know he had a lot of enemies, Paul was great at making and keeping friends – different kinds of friendships with all kinds of people.

I think we can learn something from a man like this today. These people are not "Facebook friends" for Paul – a mixture of close but also very tenuous relationships! He knows and is known, loves and is loved, cares and is cared for, prays and is prayed for.

The Bible is a spiritual book, but it is also a very practical book and I want to get into the nuts and bolts as we look at this together. I am going to go through various types of friendships and ask you to think deeply about your own relationships, not asking, "Have I got a friend like that?" but, "Am I a friend like that? Who am I being a friend like that to? Who could I be a friend like that to?"

"When we honestly ask ourselves which person in our lives means the most to us, we often find that it is those who, instead of giving much advice, solutions, or cures, have chosen rather to share our pain and touch our wounds with a gentle and tender hand. The friend who can be silent with us in a moment of despair or confusion, who can stay with us in an hour of grief and bereavement, who can tolerate not knowing, not curing, not healing and face with us the reality of our powerlessness, that is a friend who cares."
—Henri Nouwen, *Out of Solitude*

PUT YOUR LIFE ON THE LINE

Near the top of single Paul's list are a married couple called Priscilla and Aquila. Paul says they risked their lives for him. I don't know any detail about what that heroism involved, but that's one of the deepest levels of loving friendship. There are only a few men I could say that about in my own experience from my days in the cops. One of them, "Big Johnny" remains my best friend. He's the kind of bloke Elbert Hubbard must have been thinking of when he wrote his definition of a friend, "The man who knows all about you, and still likes you." Putting your life on the line for someone is an extraordinary measure of friendship.

The first time I heard the Bible's message explained in a way I could relate to was when a preacher called Eric Delve held a nail in the air, saying, "This is a Roman nail. This is the kind of nail that would have been driven into Jesus' hands and feet. If someone had to have a nail driven into them, who do you love enough that you would say, 'Don't do it to them, do it to me instead?'"

At the time I was far from God. I didn't even believe he existed. I was only there for the girl who'd invited me, but it was an interesting question and my mind whirred. I went through a list to see who would make the cut:

The girl who'd brought me to hear the speaker? Gorgeous, but no. I hardly knew her at the time (now we're married and I'd give a different answer).

My Dad? No – he's a lot tougher than me, he could handle it better.

My brother? (We weren't getting on that well at the time). No. Leave him to it.

My sister? Maybe.

Finally, I picked one person I was sure of. My Mum. I'd do it for my Mum.

The place was packed but the speaker seemed to look me right in the eye now as he said, "If you picked anyone, it would have to be someone who you really loved. Jesus did it for you. He said he was doing this for you, because of your sins. He was taking the punishment you deserve so you could be forgiven. That nail shows how much God loves you."

And I was nailed by that statement.

I'd heard the basics of the gospel message since being a child, but I had rejected what I thought it was. "Jesus died for the sins of the world." So what? Irrelevant. I knew from the Police there are a lot of bad people in the world. Hearing such a message probably comforted people, I thought. I hoped it didn't comfort the worst who deserved all they got. I wasn't sad, bad or needy. I never thought I needed God's love. Until the moment when it was explained in those terms.

Now, it was personal. This wasn't about the sins of the world but the sins of Anthony Delaney. The offer of new life and forgiveness, from being an enemy of God to being a friend – that offer had my name on it. I could accept or reject this love. But ignoring it was no longer an option, because now I'd finally begun to understand it.

I somehow managed to shrug the power of that challenge off for a while, but the fact that I recall it so clearly decades later, the reason the message hit me so hard, was that I really did know what it is to have friends willing to lay down their life for you. It didn't apply to everyone – many would rather stay safe, thanks very much. But some of the blokes I worked closely with – Mark, John, Tony – between us was an unspoken bond, forged by going through some hairy scary times together. Kicking people's doors down and having crossbow bolts fired at you or fighting alongside someone at a football match or in a pub with everyone throwing pint pots at you lets you know who your mates are.

Priscilla and Aquila had, at some point, gone to that level for Paul. Risking their lives. I don't know if anyone other than Jesus has ever done it for you, but to get to that point in a relationship it must have started somewhere.

I don't know who you would be willing to risk or even lay down your life for. Perhaps that'll help you think now about your own inner circle, but any friendship has to start somewhere. We can read how Paul first connected with Priscilla and Aquila in the book of Acts, chapter 18, when Paul was a stranger in the city of Corinth.

You can read the whole experience for yourself, but I'll highlight a few passages as we go through and see if you agree with me that as we look at the various friendships Paul developed and enjoyed, the key to them was *sharing*.

"Paul left Athens and went to Corinth. There he met a Jew named Aquila, a native of Pontus, who had recently come from Italy with his wife Priscilla, because Claudius had ordered all the Jews to leave Rome. Paul went to see them, and because he was a tentmaker as they were, he stayed and worked with them." (Acts 18:1-3)

SHARED EXPERIENCE

Various things we can share can build and strengthen our relationships. These guys had a shared experience. They had recently come to this large, wealthy city from different places in the Roman empire – strangers in town with different accents. Paul had recently arrived, so had they. A shared experience. Not much of a connection, but enough for Paul to build on.

Paul made the first move. That's important to notice! Sometimes we sit around waiting for everyone to come and befriend us but I believe, by the grace of God, even the shyest person can learn to be the first to walk across the room and extend a hand of friendship, kick off a conversation, remember a name, pay attention, ask questions to draw out the other person (like Disraeli must have done rather than talk about himself) and find common ground – rather than expecting someone to do it to us. Be a friend like that!

Their shared experience included the fact that they were both going through a similar tough time. Paul later wrote that when he arrived in Corinth it was "with fear and trembling". Wherever Paul went he divided opinion. He kicked over fences people wanted to sit on and as a result often went from one kind of trouble to a different sort of bother, particularly with the authorities. Priscilla and Aquila had just been thrown out of Rome because the Emperor was disturbed by the fear of riots, as so many Jews were turning to follow one they called "Chrestus".

They had a Jewish heritage and we don't know whether Priscilla and Aquila were also Christians before they met Paul or not, but they did have some things in common. Not everything, but enough. When you are looking for friendships it is good to look at what you have in common, don't just focus on the differences. Paul was single, they were married. Maybe they were different ages. They originated from different countries. It is good to mix it up a little! Single people: don't just focus on having have single friends! Married people: don't just have married friends! Mix it up. They had shared experiences and common ground.

SHARED WORK

They had something else in common. Paul was a tent maker as they were. He stayed and worked with them. They became business partners.

Studies from the Department of Obvious Facts show that working environments where people feel they are engaged in tasks together with *friends* rather than just *colleagues* are less stressful and more productive. (Okay, I made this one up, but I wouldn't be surprised if someone did pay someone else inordinate amounts of money to prove it!)

Do you have friends in the workplace? Sometimes you can have great friendships at work if you show you are a man of integrity, honesty and someone who isn't going to badmouth and gossip like everyone else. If you can be relied on at work, too, people want a friend like that. Walt Whitman wrote a poem which summarizes the way to success at work and friendship:

There is man in the world who never gets turned down,
Wherever he chances to stray;
He gets the glad hand in the populous town,
Or out where the farmers make hay;
He is greeted with pleasure on deserts of sand,
And deep in the aisles of the woods;
Wherever he goes there is a welcoming hand
- He's the man who delivers the goods.

SHARED HOME

The three even shared a home together, which can either make or break a friendship! Over the years our family has been incredibly enriched by opening up our home to have various people and even whole families coming to live with us, some just for a short time and some for several months.

Of course you don't have to have everyone come and live with you, but how about inviting some people round for a meal or getting the barbecue going in the famous British summer? Even if you can't cook, every man can barbecue!

The Bible encourages us that when we open up our home like this, we could find we're "entertaining angels unawares" and though I don't think we ever had any angels, we got some great friends as a result (usually!) – people who have stayed the course over many years. Silas and Timothy were friends like this to Paul:

"When Silas and Timothy came from Macedonia, Paul devoted himself exclusively to preaching, testifying to the Jews that Jesus was the Christ." (Acts 18:5)

SHARED PASSION

Paul's work was as a tentmaker. But that was just his job. It wasn't the only thing he was interested in. It was not what he lived for.

Now his old mates turned up in town. They had been delayed while he'd been in another city. Silas had been in a Macedonian prison with Paul, not because they were jail-birds but because they had been arrested for preaching, since it was considered illegal. They had even been through an earthquake together.

When you have been through an earthquake with some-body you end up becoming better friends. I was recently privileged to go to the grief-stricken island of Haiti with my pal, Andy Hawthorne, founder and director of The Message, to bring emergency medical aid and food packages to field hospitals within days of the terrible earthquake which killed hundreds of thousands and displaced millions.

Andy I went through earthquake tremors, aftershocks, every day we were out there. On one occasion it happened when Andy was sitting on the loo! The whole building started to shake and we'd been told wherever you were inside, if it starts to shake, you have got a maximum of fifteen seconds to get out. He was reaching for the door handle and still debating whether to pull his trousers up when the tremor stopped, thankfully! I know he'll be grateful that I shared that story with you. It's what friends are for.

Australian poet John Leonard says, "It takes a long time to grow an old friend." Paul and Silas had a past together and they shared a passion for the gospel. Andy and I have known each as acquaintances for twenty years or more, but it is only spending time together in extreme circumstances that connected us deeper. We have a shared passion to connect ordinary people, and especially the poorest of the poor, to the life-changing God who loves them. A previous visit when we went together with our wives to Haiti a year before the quake cemented that, then going through a time when the whole world wobbles and you're utterly dependent on God for shelter, protection and miraculous provision (and finding how He comes through for you with the miracles you need) only increases the friendship and desire to make a difference in the world with this one short life.

SHARED MENTORING

Timothy was a younger guy who Paul was intentionally mentoring. They had become very close, though a generation or two apart. Paul had been mentoring Priscilla and Aquila too, but he calls Timothy his "son" – he treats him like one, and invests in his life.

So many younger men are longing for older guys who'd be willing to open up their hearts, homes, diaries and lives for them – sharing not just their successes, but the times when they have struggled and made a bad decision! They want to know how others who have gone before them learned, overcame and carried on.

If only more older men were willing to share such life lessons, I could fill a stadium with younger guys longing for that. Our society could be transformed by a mentoring movement like that. It's the key to holistic life success.

So many young men are literally dying for lack of someone to pray for them, believe in them, speak a timely word of encouragement to them. You can't do that with everybody and neither can I, but are you doing that with anyone? I have a small group of guys I mentor and I am also mentored by a number of older men who have walked the road further and better than me. As a younger person, are you looking and asking for somebody older who you can do that with? If you are an older man, who are you pouring your life into in that way? If you can love, you can mentor.

It's good that Paul has friends like this because as you read on you'll see that when he preaches in Corinth it doesn't go too well. He has friends, but he also has some enemies, who become abusive. There are lots of people who like me, I am pleased to say. But I know there are also some people who don't like me (I can live with that, I don't even like me sometimes!) Paul wasn't intentionally going round and making enemies, but he had learnt how to cope with it. In my previous book, *The (Don't Have) To Do List*, I wrote a chapter called, "I Don't Have to Worry if Someone Rejects Me." Have you learned that lesson, which Paul teaches us again here? He didn't stop trying to make friends because he had been rejected by some people. What did he do?

> *"Then Paul left the synagogue and went next door to the house of Titius Justus, a worshiper of God. Crispus, the synagogue ruler, and his entire household believed in the Lord; and many of the Corinthians who heard him believed and were baptized."* (Acts 18:7-8)

SHARED NEIGHBORHOOD

Somebody might reject you, but there's often somebody sitting right next to them looking for a friend like you! We are just not looking in the right place. The next set of great friends were right next-door to Paul! They shared the neighborhood together.

Some people sit around wishing they had loads of friends, but don't go and initiate any friendships, even with the people next door. Paul had put forward a revolutionary idea just a short time before when he'd visited Athens. The idea was this: that where you live right now is no accident – it is God's plan! Paul said that as God distributed people around the world and throughout history he, *"... determined the times set for them and the exact places where they should live. God did this so that men would seek him and perhaps reach out for him and find him, though he is not far from each one of us."*

This tells me that there are people living on my street, or moving in soon, for this reason: so that I get to share something of my life with them. They live on my street right now, so I can help them as they reach out to connect with the God who is reaching out to them. I don't do this by putting "Jesus loves you" posters in my windows, but just by being the best possible neighbor I can be.

Recently, my father-in-law told me that he'd bumped into a guy who used to live opposite me years ago. I was always friendly with this bloke – but that was mainly because I knew he was a professional boxer and a bit of a scary character. In fact, I didn't even know his name, I just used to call him Boss! But when he met my father-in-law he said, "Are you related to Anthony? Anthony Delaney?" He bravely admitted that was the case.

"Tell him I'm a Christian now," he said. "I never was when he was my neighbor, but now I am. And tell him, I will never forget what he said to me that day when I was washing my car."

I'm glad he'll never forget what I said to him that day, because I certainly can't remember! I don't even remember the conversation. But I do remember we both shared a neighborhood, and we must have shared a moment that God used to draw him to himself.

SHARED JOURNEY

"Paul stayed on in Corinth for some time. Then he left the brothers and sailed for Syria, accompanied by Priscilla and Aquila ... They arrived at Ephesus, where Paul left Priscilla and Aquila. He himself went into the synagogue and reasoned with the Jews. When they asked him to spend more time with them, he declined. But as he left, he promised, 'I will come back if it is God's will.'" (Acts 18:18-21)

The trouble got worse and then a little better in Corinth before Paul moved on, but he was not alone. Priscilla and Aquila shared the journey. Then he left them.

There are some people you share the journey with and you become friends along the way. Then you say goodbye, and that's okay. There are some people I have been friends with for a while, good friends, close friends – and then they or I have gone off on a different part of the journey. Their life has gone in one direction and mine has gone in another and that is okay, we can still be friends. I don't have to get all rejected and hurt about that. I don't have to say they abandoned me. People come and people go. I don't own anyone and they don't owe me anything.

SHARED TIME

Paul shared his time with some new people at Ephesus, but then there came a point when he knew he'd spent enough time with them, so when they wanted more from him he said, "Thanks, but no." Paul was a busy guy, with demands from all kinds of people asking him to stay with them, so sometimes he said no. Sometimes we have to say no even to good people and good things in order to do God's best for us.

Are you any good at saying no? Paul said, "You know what? This has been great, but I'm off now. If it's God's will, I will come back." He didn't stay there with them just to keep them smiling another day, at the expense of doing what he really should have been doing with his time. Jesus did the same kind of thing. The crowds had been pressing round him and so he went of to pray a while on his own. Look what happened:

> *"At daybreak Jesus went out to a solitary place. The people were looking for him and when they came to where he was, they tried to keep him from leaving them. But he said, 'I must preach the good news of the kingdom of God to the other towns also, because that is why I was sent.'"* (Luke 4:42-43)

Jesus said no to people.

I need to know how to say no better and I bet you do too. I need to learn to say, "Maybe, if it is God's will, we'll do that at some point – but not now." Like everybody else I have 1,440 minutes in this day and there are things I need to do and things I don't need to do.

Most of us are uncomfortable saying no and suffer for it. How can we improve? I read an interview way back with a movie star – I think it was Paul Newman, but don't hold me to it – where he was asked the most important lesson he'd ever learned. He said it was to be able to say "No" well. He said he used a phrase when he was invited to do something he really shouldn't be doing: "I'm sorry, but that's impossible for me." He found that people didn't tend to argue with this phrase and persist in asking. Now, I believe it's true that nothing is impossible for God, but I also need to know I can't do everything or please everyone, so I've used that little phrase time and again since I read it. It's got me out of a world of hassle many times, so I pass it on!

In order to be able to concentrate on the things that God is calling me to do, this is what I need to do. Say no. Nicely, politely, firmly. "No". When we learn to say to some things and people we can say "yes" where it's really important and build relationships, as Paul did, that have a positive ripple effect. Look at this example:

> *"Meanwhile a Jew named Apollos, a native of Alexandria, came to Ephesus. He was a learned man, with a thorough knowledge of the Scriptures. He had been instructed in the way of the Lord, and he spoke with great fervor and taught about Jesus accurately, though he knew only the baptism of John. He began to speak boldly in the synagogue. When Priscilla and Aquila heard him, they invited him to their home and explained to him the way of God more adequately."* (Acts 18:24-26)

When Paul left Priscilla and Aquila, he left something them with them! We know this because we see that when an extraordinarily gifted man with some holes in his thinking and theology later turned up in their orbit, Priscilla and Aquila make the first move. They went to him, welcomed him into their home, and lovingly straightened him out on a few things. They looked at the Bible together and discussed important issues to help Apollos grow to be all he could be and do all he was meant to do for God. Where did this sharing, this mentoring come from? It had rubbed off on them from Paul. It was the return on what Paul had invested in them.

Apollos couldn't have been the man he became without that which his friends, Priscilla and Aquila, invested in him. And they couldn't have done that had it not been for Paul and the deposit he made in their lives back in Corinth. Emerson wrote that a man's growth is seen in the successive choirs of his friends. This is the way it should work.

Later on, Paul wrote to a different church, *"We loved you so much that we were delighted to share with you not only the gospel of God but our lives as well, because you had become so dear to us"* (1 Thessalonians 2:8).

What would the Church look like to the world if that were increasingly true of its people? It is possible to share the message of God's love with somebody and not to share anything of your life, because it happens all the time.

Paul wanted not just to share knowledge, but his life too. He shared experiences, work and home, he shared a passion for his life mission, matched only by his desire to share what mattered most to him with the next generation. Paul encouraged people, he spent time with people, he said no to some people so that he could say yes to other people, he mentored people, he invested in people. Is it any wonder he had friends? I wish I could be a friend like that!

CLOSER THAN A BROTHER

If you were to as Paul, even though he had all sorts of friendships going on, that playground question, "Who's your best friend?" You know who he would say, don't you?

Jesus.

Of course.

Proverbs calls him the friend, *"who sticks closer than a brother."* If you read through the whole of chapter 18 in Acts you'd know that Paul had a hard time in Corinth. People rejected him and abused him. He was scared and very lonely, at the end of his tether, perhaps wondering if he was in the right place at all.

It's said a friend walks in when everyone else walks out. Ever heard that? On that awful night, Paul's best friend walked in:

> *"One night the Lord spoke to Paul in a vision: 'Do not be afraid; keep on speaking, do not be silent. For I am with you, and no one is going to attack and harm you, because I have many people in this city.'"* (Acts 18:9-10)

What a friend we have in Jesus! He told him he was with him and was protecting him. We have friends who come and go throughout our lives, but I have a friend who sticks closer than a brother. I have a friend who promises, "I won't leave you or forsake you, and I say YES to you, I want you to be my best friend. And once you say "yes" to me and I say "yes" to you, it doesn't matter who might say "no" to you any more! The friendship is sealed. I will never reject you, abandon you or leave you alone. I am with you always – so don't be afraid."

Isn't that fantastic? Jesus makes that promise to you. That offer. Who is your best friend? Jesus says he wants to be your best friend. That is the vulnerable moment. He became ultimately vulnerable on the cross for you, stretched out his arms wide for a God-man-hug. Will you come and be his friend? Will you go and befriend others with that same kind of vulnerable love?

That is such an amazing promise! *"Do not be afraid ... because I am with you."* Jesus makes that promise to you and to me. Will you be his best friend? He will be yours.

I remember years ago talking to kids in a secondary school class RE lesson, trying to explain the gospel as best as I could – the whole of it, in the half an hour they'd given me. A girl sitting at the back chewing gum like you are not supposed to, put a hand up, looking very unimpressed. "So you're telling me, right, that the Bible says, right, that God really, really loves us and wants to be our friend?" She was smirking by the end, as if this was the most ridiculous message ever! All I could say was, "Yes," because she had summed it up perfectly.

Karl Barth, one of the greatest theologians ever, with a brain the size of a planet, who wrote massive books on theology, came on a tour to the USA and was asked, "Doctor Barth, after all you have written and studied, what is the most important insight?"

He replied, "Jesus loves me, this I know, for the Bible tells me so."

That's it. Jesus wants to be your friend, forever. To quote a Meerkat: "Simples!"

Father
Fitness
Friends
JESUS
Finances
Family
Failures

"Look, the thing about my family is there's five of us: Marge, Bart, Girl Bart, the one who doesn't talk and the fat guy.
How I loathe him."

—Homer (Simpson)

SIX

Family

[the most important thing about family]

How many of the following are real titles of Country and Western songs?

Mama Get The Hammer (There's A Fly On Papa's Head).

Her Teeth Was Stained, But Her Heart Was Pure.

How Can I Miss You, If You Won't Go Away?

I Changed Her Oil, She Changed My Life.

I Don't Know Whether To Kill Myself Or Go Bowling.

I Don't Want Your Body If Your Heart's Not In It.

I've Got Tears In My Ears From Lying On My Back In My Bed While I Cry Over You.

Get Your Tongue Outta My Mouth, 'Cause I'm Kissing You Goodbye.

If The Phone Don't Ring, Baby, You'll Know It's Me.

I'll get onto the answer and the tenuous reason for the quiz later.

THE MOST IMPORTANT THING ABOUT FAMILY

I was once asked at short notice to write an article for a men's magazine on the subject of family. I love to write, but the deadline was just a couple of days away. We were getting ready to go away on a short family holiday.

I wanted to say yes. They say the main secret to being a writer is to apply glue to your backside and get in the chair until you finish writing. I decided I could squeeze the time in to write the article, along with all the other things I had to do for work, before the holiday.

All it would take was less helping at home, less time with Zoe and the kids, more stress for myself and everyone else, offloading more pressure on my team and locking myself in the study because I was doing "the work of the Lord". I could probably even angle it so they'd all feel guilty if they tried interrupting such important work – I'm a master at that.

But the subject defeated me: *Family*.

I remembered how close I came to losing my family through just such shenanigans years ago. I nearly wrecked my life chasing a qualification nobody cares about. I emailed the editor: "Sorry mate, but I can't do it." That was very hard for me to do – a man who, like you, wants to feel needed, important and significant. To press send on an email admitting to not actually being able to do everything is hard. It was tough to say no, especially to a friend. It was hard to say no to more of "God's work" in order to say "yes" to family time.

The fact is, I can quantify how many hours I put into my job, but I can't quantify how well I'm doing as a Dad or as a husband. Perhaps that's why many blokes end up putting their all into their work, laying everything on that altar, because it all "counts" somehow. Whereas we never really know how well we're doing in the area of family. There's no tick sheet for that.

"Why is it I can have huge energy at work, but want to collapse when I get home, just when my two daughters most want to speak to me? I've learned the hard way, after one day seeing disappointment in their eyes, to get over myself. My family were always my priority in my head and heart and now they are in my actions as well."
—Carl Beech

Despite the email refusal, the subject of family still ticked away in the back of my mind. Because I wasn't writing an article about family I could sit down with mine for a meal that day, so I asked my son and daughter, "What do you think the most important thing about family is?"

Joel said, "You should all trust each other enough to tell each other what you are thinking, whatever that is." The fact that he said it, proved to me he does. Fantastic!

What Hannah said was, in my opinion, really quite profound, showing what a huge amount of emotional intelligence she has been gifted with. After a few moments thought, she volunteered, "I think the most important thing about families is that we need to remember that the other people in the family are, themselves, people, not just roles."

I asked her to explain that a little. "Well," she said, "it's only been in the last couple of years that I've come to realize you're not just 'my Dad' and Mum's not just 'my Mum'.

You're separate people with your own ideas, and lives, and everything."

Wow! How often have I thought of her as "Hannah Delaney" instead of "my daughter"? Not enough.

TREE PEOPLE

One day Jesus healed a blind man. He took him away from the crowd so he could give him his undivided, individual attention, then prayed for him. Then he asked if the man could see.

He said, "I see people like trees, walking around."

Now I have to admit, if it had been the Anthony Delaney Traveling Ministry Healing Crusade, I'd have called that a result! I might have passed the collection plate, got everyone's credit card details and charged an extortionate amount to send out my miracle hankies! (Do not get me started on Christian TV).

Jesus wasn't satisfied.

My wife calls me, "Half a job Joe". I kid myself it's affectionate. She says it because of all the part-completed projects I am surrounded by, especially DIY (which when I make things, stands for Drat! Idiot! Yelling!)

Jesus, master carpenter of Nazareth, is NOT a half-a-job kind of guy. He wasn't happy that the blind man only saw people looking like trees. Jesus wanted him to see other people as PEOPLE! Like my Hannah does. So He prayed for him again. I believe we men need that second touch from Jesus, so we can see people as people, however our family is constituted.

Sometimes (too often when I'm in a rush) people – even those closest to me who I'm supposed to love the most – end up, well, camouflaged. I can't see them for the trees. I'm all too easily allured, distracted, self-focused. Such a blurred and myopic focus is dangerous to me and my family.

DEAL OR NO DEAL?

James (not his real name) used to be in marketing until he got into gambling. Highly intelligent and creative, he was on more money than any of his peers until about ten years ago. One night, after a brainstorming session for another "great new product" we all ought to rush out and buy, his brain was all stormed out. A few of the blokes were going off to a casino, so he decided to join them. He won big that night and that was all it took. He was hooked. He didn't even fight it. The buzz was too strong. But never quite strong enough. There was always the promise of more! So he went on looking.

He didn't literally put his kids on the table and see them spin off, but he might as well have done. Nobody who shares his surname would now give him the time of day. He lost his girlfriend and had a lot of one night stands. After a while he cut out the chat-up lines altogether and just paid for sex, as and when.

James likes the music in my church and he likes the people because they like him, but he still likes crack cocaine best. I've talked with him a few times about what he thinks about God and he says, "God loves me anyway." He told me drugs aren't bad, they are "nice". That's all that matters to him.

I'd not seen him for ages, then he came to my front door. He was going to wait for a bus and he'd missed one because he couldn't even start to run for it. I wouldn't have let him on my bus if I'd been a driver. He's my age but looks twenty years older (and I'm looking rough as I write this).

He told me where he'd been. On a super binge.

The last item of value he'd owned from his former life was a little flat. He'd sold it just after Christmas and spent the tens of thousands it released on a "bender" of hard drugs and warm prostitutes. He'd spent months of living like hell, so no wonder he looked like it. The bus would take him to a squat where someone was letting him have a sofa.

"So now you've got nothing?"

The black teeth showed widely. "Well, I've always got God haven't I?"

He's only ever got that part of the message, so far, the grace side. Enough to save you for the next life, but not enough to make any difference at all in this one. He knows enough to somehow understand he's loved, but he hasn't opened himself up so that the love can change his life.

I've prayed with a number of people during their deathbed conversions. Maybe you're reading this and that's your plan too? Live like hell till the end, then ask forgiveness and secure a place in heaven with your last breath. If God is real he has to forgive you, right? I mean, it's his job after all. I have news for you in the final chapter about that.

"God loves me anyway, Anthony."

I had to go some way toward agreeing with James, theologically, but I wanted to smack him one (I know that's not a pastorally sensitive response. How did they ever let me slip through the net?) I didn't wait for the next bus with him. I was too brassed off.

I couldn't get him out of my mind – the waste! The waste of money in a world of need. The waste of potential. The waste of a life. The waste of his family. It still burned inside me next day as I woke, and then God challenged my thinking. I've found that reading the Bible regularly does that.

SMOKE AND MIRRORS

I read about a king, Solomon, the wisest and richest man who'd ever lived to that point, so they say – the man who had everything. But he came up empty too. He started on a quest to try to find fulfillment by self-gratification and he had the means to do it big time. I'm glad he wrote about his experience so we can learn from it.

> *"I said to myself, 'Let's go for it—experiment with pleasure, have a good time!' But there was nothing to it, nothing but smoke. What do I think of the fun-filled life? Insane! Inane! My verdict on the pursuit of happiness? Who needs it?"*
>
> *Everything I wanted I took—I never said no to myself. I gave in to every impulse, held back nothing. I sucked the marrow of pleasure ...*
>
> *Then I took a good look at everything I'd done ... when I looked, I saw nothing but smoke. Smoke and spitting into the wind. There was nothing to any of it. Nothing."*

I realized that what James had done in those months since Christmas is just what lots of us men do, but usually to a lesser degree and over a longer period of time.

He decided to live selfishly, as if the man in the mirror was all that mattered. He figured he would live according to however he felt at the time. He put himself at the centre of his world and wanted everything and everyone else to spin round him. At various times the Bible says God wants us to love others, "as ourselves". Most men are pretty good at loving themselves. A woman passes her reflection and finds fault with her hair or outfit. A man glimpses himself and thinks, "Oh yeah! I've still got it!" We are entranced by ourselves in a culture that encourages and affirms our narcissism. But how good would your family say you are at loving them as much as you love yourself?

Men who consider Christian marriage are challenged to do what is most alien and foreign to our masculine nature, so we'll know that we have to receive the help of heaven to do it. Here's a high call: to sacrifice, to put the other first. One of the most regular wedding readings originates from a time and society which encouraged men to treat women as an underclass and wives as chattels. The apostle Paul would have stunned those who first read the maker's instructions for building a strong family, and it's still stings like a wet slap two thousand years on:

> *"Husbands, love your wives, just as Christ loved the church and gave himself up for her ... In this same way, husbands ought to love their wives as their own bodies. After all, no one ever hated his own body, but he feeds and cares for it."*

Men know how to feed and care for ourselves. Alright, just point me to a kebab shop! That perfectly good and natural process can show us how we should care for others too. But there's something gone wrong in the deepest part of our souls which needs to be surrendered back to the one who made us, or else it twists to selfishness, greed and pride.

Selfishness and craving for instant gratification (get a buzz now and forget about tomorrow) takes control until men whose "god is their stomach" spread out a wasted life in any number of ways over years and decades. James was just doing it on fast forward with the volume turned right up. But at least he was honest about it.

There are other much quieter and more deceptive ways to waste this life too, which look to most of us a lot more like success than failure until you get up close. I don't know how many hundreds of funerals I've performed, but one man's still haunts my memory. A rich man.

THE RICH GHOST

I parked next to the Bentley as I went to meet the undertaker at the huge mansion just a few doors down from the Premiership footballer. This man had been a captain of industry. He owned businesses and properties on three continents, but following my conversation with the funeral director, it became apparent that there would only be a solicitor at the service to act as executor. (In the end I managed to push a few neighbors who didn't know him into coming too, so the place wouldn't feel so empty. I'm an extrovert!) What could I say at the graveside I wondered.

> "Children don't remember days, they remember moments."
> —Steve Legg (Sorted Magazine)

SUCCESSFUL?

This man had successfully alienated, hurt and pushed away several former wives and the children he had no time for in this life. So much so that none of them would even come and see him buried. That doesn't look to me like a life well lived.

James and this man serve as two extreme examples, for sure, but there is a pattern. There is a temptation particularly shaped for each man, that will lead, by a series of broad downward steps rather than a sudden cliff-top drop, not only to separation from God, but to a relational life that ends up looking like a bad country and western song (by the way, *all* those titles were real attempts at chart success).

If an impartial, wise observer were to speak into the life of James, Solomon, or the rich guy, do you know what they'd say? "Don't live like that! Don't do it!"

We recognize that our choices and decisions can make a massive difference to whether family will be something we enjoy or endure, rejoice in or regret. Reading our papers we clearly see coal men destroying their families. Shaking our heads we say we don't know how they could be so stupid: "Hey, Wayne Rooney, Tiger Woods (insert alternative name of bozo from your paper today)! Why are you making such ridiculous choices? Can't you see the world of pain you're heading toward? It's obvious!"

The writer of Proverbs asks a rhetorical question that demands the obvious answer: "Duh!"

"Can a man scoop fire into his lap without his clothes being burned?"

Can we cheat on our wives by making sex, work or sport our mistress and not end up getting burned? No – it's obvious.

Can we make more and more decisions that leave us with less and less time to spend with our children and not end up with them saying one day that they have no time for us? No – it's obvious.

It's like watching Jack Bauer on 24. Many times watching the series I shouted at the screen, "No Jack! Oh, this is ridiculous! Why would you do that? It's all going to blow up in your face! Don't open that door!" At such times I'm grateful that my wife kindly reminds me, "It's not a documentary."

We all know guys who started out well. We looked up to them. They were the last guy we expected to go wrong, but now they've crashed and burned. The shrapnel is sticking out of their "should-have-been loved ones". They lost everything that they would say was most important to them and caused irreparable damage because of what were ultimately "trivial pursuits". If we were able to look on from the stands at various pivotal moments and see the mess they were making of their relationships and how they were screwing up their families, we would say, "It's going to end in tears! It's not worth it!"

That office conversation which led to a flirtatious remark and a lingering touch ... if having played the movie forward you could witness the tragedy or farce it all becomes, if you could pause the "life tape" there, you'd want to rewind and make a very different choice.

It seems so obvious in other men's lives. How come we're so blind to it in our own – the little things that lead to big problems?

DISCOVERY

The space shuttle *Discovery* was grounded recently. Not by complex technical difficulties, but by Yellow-shafted flicker woodpeckers. The birds found the insulating foam on the shuttle's external fuel tank irresistible for pecking. Without the foam, ice forms on the tank when it is filled with the super-cold fuel – ice that can break free during lift-off and damage the giant spacecraft.

Years filled with tense hours, sitting in airless rooms, trying to hold marriages and families together have shown me that these most important of human relationships are frequently damaged not only by big and obvious things, such as adultery, abuse and abandonment, but by little things.

Do you know the best way to bury a marriage? Lots of little digs! Criticism, lack of respect, taking each other for granted, all peck away and keep us from reaching the heights. Focusing on the negatives will only develop misery.

Do I try to fix what's wrong or just fix the blame? I could rehearse and remember everything that's ever gone wrong in my relational life. But if I just dwelt on those difficulties, before long I'd be curled in the corner of the room in a foetal position. Or else, I can take a different tack.

Management guru Marcus Buckingham wrote a fascinating book, *The One Thing You Need To Know*. It is, of course, a business book, though what grabs me most is not what he writes about the workplace, but about what it takes to have a happy marriage. He points out something he maintains is the most important thing to know about being happily married. Basically, it's about focusing on the positives, even accentuating them in the other person. We need to positively discriminate for one another. Whatever happens, Buckingham says, "Find the most generous explanation for each other's behavior and believe it."

Imagine how much stronger our families would be if we made a decision to see the best in each other, speak the best of each other, believe the best of each other?

Oh, you say, but I don't know your situation. And sure, I've never met your mother-in-law ...

How bad can family get? It's a matter of perspective.

Once upon a time, a man lived with his wife, two small children, and his elderly parents in a tiny hut. He tried to be patient and gracious, but the noise and crowded conditions wore him down. In desperation, he consulted the village wise man.

"Keep a cockerel in the hut too," the wise man said, "then come see me again next week."

The next week, the man returned and told the wise elder that his living conditions were worse than ever, with all the crowing and mess in the hut. "Do you have a cow?" asked the wise elder.

The man nodded fearfully. "Take your cow into the hut as well, and come see me in a week."

Over the next several weeks, the man, on the advice of the wise elder, made room for a goat, two dogs, and all his brother's children.

Finally, he could take no more, and in a fit of anger, kicked out all the animals and guests, leaving only his wife, his children, and his parents. Then he realized that, suddenly, his home had become spacious and quiet.

Thank God for your family – they are the ones God meant to live with you!

THE DYSFUNCTIONAL FAMILY OF GOD

If you want to start reading what God thinks about family, you don't have to read too far into the Bible. Right near the front in Genesis it tells us that "family" was God's idea, created to be the building block for a strong society. Having declared everything "good", God made Adam and said, "Very good!"

But God then said, *"It is **not** good ... for man to be alone. I will make a helper suitable for him."* Notice this: here's a man, our prototype bloke, in the perfect environment, with a great job (if you're the outdoor type) and the perfect boss. He's at the head of the food chain, the top of the tree (couldn't resist that one).

But God said, "It's not good for that man to be alone."

That's still true whether you're married or a single man. You were made for relationship. It's a basic need, like air, water and pizza. We need relationships. Man was not made to be alone, so God created the first human family. He addressed Adam's aloneness and met that need for companionship. Then He looked and said, "Now, it's good."

God made Eve and Adam said, "Woah! Man!" which is where the word "babe" comes from in Hebrew. It was the first marriage. But were they the perfect couple?

I've officiated at many weddings and it's surprising how often you'll hear in the speeches some reference to, "the perfect couple". There's no such thing. Not even Adam and Eve were perfect. Read on!

You may be relieved to know that this first family proved to be dysfunctional. Before long, Adam and Eve fell into temptation then fell out, each blaming the other, a reptile or even God for their problems. One of their kids killed the other one right after church, and it all went downhill from there. The generations that followed made the guests on Jerry Springer's show look like the Waltons.

GOD'S FAMILY ALBUM

But do you know what the great news is? Running alongside all of their family stories, from one problem family to the next, is God himself – sticking close, never giving up on them, working out a plan, his purpose always prevailing.

God knows that every family, every relationship, has its ups and downs. He's not in denial of that, even if we are. He is also unchanging in his promise, power and perfect love.

Like any good father, at times God sometimes has to be cruel to be kind. Often his children are at a loss to understand everything he's doing. But, when you flick through the pages of God's big family album, the story consistently portrayed is that even when God's people are unfaithful, He is always faithful. While they deserve nothing, he provides, protects and blesses. When they don't stay loving, he never stops. They feud, he forgives. When they're weak, he gives them his strength.

I love to sit and look through old family albums. Page after page of memories of laughter, occasions, holidays, people and places. I'm amazed at how the kids have grown so fast (my waistline too). I'm amazed how I thought I looked cool.

Like you, we generally only got the camera out on happy days, when we'd put our arms around each other and say "cheese", so everything in our album looks like the best days of our lives. Our family album can't possibly tell the full story. Things are even worse these days – the ubiquity of the digital camera means we don't have to wait to see whether the picture turns out how we wanted it to, like we did with those old pictures. (Some people reading this will never have known the joy of excitedly waiting for the roll of film you took during your week in Spain to come back from the developers, only to find your thumb obliterated Granddad's head). These days the mistakes are just deleted.

As you go through God's family album, it's different. You'll see that while there are some glorious shots and awesome landscapes, the portraits are not always too flattering. He isn't ashamed to show us, warts and all, the truth about his family because he has lessons to teach us for ours.

Turn a page – there smiles Abraham who tells lies about his wife, but ends up being called the father of faith.

God doesn't alter Noah's red-eye or omit to tell us about the flash that embarrassed his sons when he'd had a few too many to celebrate the Ark landing safely.

Flick on to Moses the murderer … Samson the weak strongman … David the adulterous king … Rahab the prostitute.

Page after page of broken people, fractured families. Nobody's left out or stood at the back, obscured by a big hat. Here in the Bible are the non-digitally enhanced or Photoshopped photos of a litany of needy, greedy, seedy people.

God's family. They get listed in Hebrews 11 where the heavenly Father's verdict is that he is *"not ashamed to be called their God."*

Now turn another page. No, a few more. Go back. Stop.

A picture of a baby.

Amazing!

God has stepped out of heaven and into the picture, the infinite infant! Is this the perfect family? He's not in a palace but a feeding trough. In the next shot he's comforted at the breast of a single mum, to be raised with a troubled stepfather in circumstances that mean the legitimacy of his birth will always be called into question from the stable to the grave. A jealous king wants to kill him. His parents lose him for a few days. His cousin eats locusts for lunch. His younger brothers and sisters stand around calling him crazy.

Not a perfect picture is it? Dr Martyn Lloyd-Jones said the Bible is the most honest book in the world. Why? Because God tells it like it is.

God knows it not good to be alone, so he gave us families. He says the church is supposed to be like a family too, which means we shouldn't be surprised if it also has its share of strange and annoying people we'd rather not bother with. What do you do with that? It's family: love them anyway. Our hearts grow bigger when we love them – and we can because Jesus' blood is thicker than water. It's not too late.

It's too late for the rich ghost. The time to make the change in our diaries that reflects a shift in our priorities is TODAY.

It's not too late for James. We'd been praying for him hard but I admit I was shocked when he knocked on my door again a couple of weeks back. He didn't even have enough money for bus fare, but he wasn't asking for that. He looked like Gollum on a diet, but I saw a glimpse of the man he could be again glint through some found new determination born out of despair: "I want to give up crack, gambling and smoking. I want to live Anthony."

He'd finally hit the place where the only direction you can look is up. He wanted my help to get him on a Christian program called Betel, which has written many new pages into the stories of countless others, similarly addicted, around the world. If he sees it through, there's hope for transformation, which may be the first step towards some reconciliation in his world. It's not too late.

Whatever your relational past, present or future, you have a heavenly Father who has the full picture. He sees the generations before that led to you being born. He holds hope and a bright future open in his hands. He knows there are nuts in every family tree! He knows families can be our source of greatest joy *and* pain. He knows families can be great, but that no family is perfect. Not yours. Not His. He can work with that, actually He specializes in it.

So smile.

Smile!

Wider! Say "Cheese!"

Why?

Because he wants you and yours in his album.

Father
Fitness
Friends
JESUS
Finances
Family
Failures

"By profession I am a soldier and take pride in that fact. But I am prouder – infinitely prouder – to be a father ... It is my hope that my son, when I am gone, will remember me not from the battlefield, but in the home repeating with him our simple daily prayer, 'Our Father who art in Heaven.'"

—General Douglas MacArthur

SEVEN

Father

[stone sarnies and snake fingers]

"It's like when I'm riding my motorbike into a hairpin bend," Noel told me, nursing his coffee. I knew enough not to interrupt. Looking into the cup again he went on. "You know what you have to do, lean in and keep the power on. But it's scary whenever you approach and so you're tempted to pull out of the turn. That's just how it feels!"

He was talking about making a life and eternity-changing decision to follow Jesus Christ, as he'd just seen others do by simply kneeling to pray at the foot of a large cross we'd set up there in the café.

For the last five mornings Noel had come along to the "Just Looking" sessions at the Christian conference I was teaching at. In this part of the showground we'd looked at various film clips, listened to people's real life stories and with lots of Q&A discussed what the Bible had to say about how ordinary, flawed people can connect to God.

Noel wasn't into God. He was into his motorbike. His wife was the "religious" one. Years before they'd agreed to a deal, a great compromise. She wasn't ever going to get excited about his Triumph Bonneville T140, and he wasn't interested in singing with a crowd. But if she went to his conventions and shows, he would go to hers.

Here, and at innumerable other Christian events, he sat outside the tent smoking or taking his bike to bits while she was at seminars. We had set up in the coffee area, he called in, and for some reason he was hooked on the sessions from day one. Genuine, intelligent questions followed at the end of every session. His wife couldn't believe he was there every single day. She never wanted to be pushy, loved him as he was no matter what, but she was praying very hard for the man she loved!

I asked him what scared him the most about becoming a Christian. "Well, take prayer – that whole 'Our Father' bit for a start," said Noel.

I should have guessed. I've talked to lots of guys who are "hard to reach", along with lots of atheists. You can often cut through the intellectual smokescreen and various pseudo-questions by simply asking, "What kind of relationship do you have with your Dad?" The range of responses is not very wide:

"Who? Never knew him."

"Critical, picky, impossible to please – and that would be on a good day."

"We just stay out of each other's way. It's for the best."

Your first reference point, map and compass for manhood is, or was, your father. Dead or alive, present or absent, good or bad, he colours your view of yourself, your attitude to older men, and crucially to God. Suppress it or deny it as you may, it still matters. If you couldn't connect with or trust him, that will carry over relationally and theologically. This is the bedrock of child psychology, the need for love and approval. If you never had your father directly praise you or lovingly hold you to demonstrate his approval, you will long and look for substitutes for that throughout your life.

Noel continued, looking at the cross now. "The words 'relationship' and 'dad' are an oxymoron. He was there, but not – you know what I mean? So when I hear preachers go on about Jesus, I'm interested. When you talk about that cross, I'm drawn somehow. But when you say it's all so I can come to God the Father … no ... not interested. Why would I want a God who is a Father?"

> "What comes to mind when we think about God is the most important thing about us. Were we able to extract from any man a complete answer to the question, 'What comes into your mind when you think about God?' we might predict with certainty the spiritual future of that man."
>
> —A W Tozer, *The Knowledge Of The Holy*

I just put a note out on my Facebook page asking for anyone who wanted to help me write this chapter to play word association and tell me their first reaction to the word "father". Within minutes I had a remarkable series of responses. Most, but not all, of those who responded were Christians. Let me relay a few to you:

FATHER =

Strength

Affirmer

Sat on his knee, warm, safe and protected (when I was a kid this was, mind you)

Secure

Warmth

First reaction is to smile! Then this picture of the open arms of the Father, my Heavenly Father, just waiting to gather me up in an embrace.

Fun

Gentle, Gentleman

Steadfast, reliable, protector

Solid

Sounds great doesn't it? No problem then.

But that was only the response of women.

This is by no means a scientific sample and I don't want to over-egg it (one or two of the men had some positive reactions, as I would have). A few men made jokes like "Christmas" or "Ted". But while *none* of the women's reactions was negative, the contrast with the men's list (some people emailed me rather than publicly post) was pretty stark:

FATHER =

Liar

Cheat

Absent

Evil

Just wanted him to say he's proud of me

Fear

Hangman

Distance

Authoritarian bad guy who scares the living **** out of you!

Ignoring

What the men's movement calls "the father wound" and others call "the fatherless crisis" is perhaps the biggest single challenge the Church in the West has to face if it is to stem the hemorrhaging of men from its ranks. The biblical doctrine of adoption could be its greatest way of reaching outsiders.

Jesus gave up his place in the family and came so that we could know God as Father. But earthly fathers have made that seem like the last thing any man would ever want.

"A Catholic priest I know tells of a nun who worked in a men's prison. One day, she said, a prisoner asked her to buy him a Mother's Day card for his mother. She did and the word traveled like wildfire around the prison. Deluged with requests, she called Hallmark Cards, who obliged with huge boxes of Mother's Day cards as a donation. The warden arranged for each inmate to draw a number, and they lined up through the cell blocks to get their cards. Weeks later, the nun was looking ahead on her calendar, and decided to call Hallmark again and ask for as many Father's Day cards in order to avoid another rush.
As Father's Day approached, the warden announced free cards were again available at the chapel. To the nun's surprise, not a single prisoner ever asked her for a Father's Day card."

—Gordon Dalbey, www.abbafather.com

STONE SARNIES AND SNAKE FINGERS

One day Jesus eyed a crowd he identified as "imperfect fathers". Even the best of dads would have been included in this group and, in order to contrast our inconsistencies with the reliability of God's love, he asked hypothetically, "Which of you, if his son asks for bread, will give him a stone? Or if he asks for a fish, will give him a snake?"

While I think this (together with many other of his sayings) points to Jesus' great comic timing, the picture it paints is appalling: a son looking for something he needs is offered something useless or even harmful.

Many of our dads were doing their level best (and so are we). But how many boys who came to dad looking for a hug were told he was "too busy right now" and received loneliness instead of affection, excuses instead of encouragement? Worse still (as I think of one amazing young man I'm trying to mentor right now), what if some received horrific abuse, even sexual. Many got boulders instead of bread, serpents instead of salmon.

THE WAY BACK HOME

The story is familiar: a young man has a wonderful father, but can't see it. One day he breaks dad's heart with five words: "I wish you were dead." He can't wait any longer! "Give me now my share of the inheritance I'd get then. Let my lame duck older brother stay here and look after the farm – I can't stand another day looking at fat calves and farm machinery, I was made for the city."

Rather than shout, spank or scold, the father does it! He liquidates half of his assets, converts them into cold cash and weeps as his son walks without a word.

The boy's a high roller for a while. It's all wine, women and song – and to be frank, he doesn't do much singing. But when the ventures fail, the adventure is stale and his friends bail. He ends up doing the only job he's qualified for: a farm laborer in charge of pigswill with a boss who treats the porkers better than the workers.

But one day, he shakes himself. "What am I doing here? If I went home, my dad could at least put me in charge of his pigs!"

He puts a fine speech together, rehearses the perfect tone of contrition, even thinks of a few religious phrases to spice it up, then tells his boss exactly where to stick the feed sack and gets walking.

It's a long journey home. Many days in the blazing sun, stinking from the pigs, tired out, thirsty and starving, but nobody will give him anything. Raging with thirst, nearer death than he knows, he finally sees the old place. There's noise inside from some kind of celebration, whiffs of something cooking that drive him crazy, even at this distance. He knocks on the door and his father opens it.

"Dad, I ... I'm so sorry ... I have been a fool. I've wasted it all ... I should have listened."

The old man replies, "I do not know you. You are no son of mine. I only have one son – he lives here with me and it is his birthday party we are celebrating. I had another son, a younger one, but he died years ago. Get off my porch or I'll get my gun. Go back to wherever you came from."

The door is slammed in his face.

Now, if you know anything at all about the Bible, you know that's not how the story ends. At least you think you know that's not how it ends. Once upon a time, for a very long time, the story *would* have ended like that.

The Rabbis, the religious teachers of the Law of Jesus' day used to tell that story to warn people, especially but not exclusively the kids: "Don't you ever step out of line. Don't presume on God's patience. He is a holy, stern God and his rules and laws must not be trifled with. If you want to have a relationship with him, stand straight and live right. Or else there's no way back. He's that kind of Father."

Then Jesus came, who knew the Father better, and changed the ending.

No wonder they wanted to kill him. He changed one of their best stories!

The kind of teaching religion loves was totally spoilt by grace. Jesus pictured for us a different kind of Father – a Father who leaves aside all pretence at dignity, picks up the skirts of his robes and runs (fathers then would never run, it was terribly unseemly), to hug the smelly son, ferociously kissing the apology only half mumbled off his mouth, giving him back his robe, ring and sandals – all the signs and insignia of a son. Here is a Father who does not lecture but lavishes, who does not castigate but celebrates his return.

What kind of an ending is that?!

Religion knows nothing of that kind of an ending. I love that kind of an ending. Since I became a Christ-follower I'm a sucker for it. No, before I came to know God as Father like that, I think it may have been hard-wired into me – and into you too. Which explains why some of the stories and movies that most pull at our hearts are excerpts or remakes of that old script.

> "If our sense of significance derives from sonship ... we will be able to achieve God's purpose for our lives."
>
> —Mark Stibbe, *From Orphans To Heirs*

Let me share something with you. It's not the kind of thing blokes normally share, but by now maybe we're closer than we were at page one, you and I. It's about what makes me cry.

When I was about seven, I sat with my Mum and watched a film on TV called *Shenandoah*. It's what I used to think of as a Saturday afternoon film, one of those indeterminably long epics that lasted right up until sponge pudding and custard, before the wrestling finished and the football results came on ("Forfar five … East Fife four"!)

Have you seen it? James Stewart plays Charlie Anderson, a landowner with six sons. The American civil war looms closer to his Southern homestead and despite his determination to protect them, his family – his boys – are inexorably drawn into the conflict, one by one.

Various intertwined plots play out, one of which involves the youngest son, known only as "Boy", who is mistakenly taken prisoner. Anderson sets off to look for him and bring him back, but the son is lost, pressed into fighting in the conflict before being shot in a battle.

All afternoon goes by and the sponge pudding knocks in the pan as the film draws to a close at another of his son's wedding. The shadow of Boy's absence hangs over the celebrations. Until ... the church doors burst open! What's this? Unbelievable! On crutches, not dead – alive! The lost son! He's here! The father sets off running.

I set off crying. Bawling. I was in bits. I'll never forget the first time I saw that film and how much I cried and my Mum never let me forget either.

When I was sixteen it was on again. I thought I could handle it now. I did, until the church doors burst open ... and then I cried like a girl in pigtails.

I'm in my mid twenties, married now, working as a cop on a tough inner city beat, soon going to be on the riot squad.

Flicking through the channels at home I say, "Guess what, Zoe? This film that's on, *Shenandoah*, I watched it when I was a kid. Ha! It used to make me cry. Let's watch it."

Bad move. Very bad move.

I now know to stay well away from that film if I want to retain my masculine composure.

But then *Finding Nemo* got me too, nearly as bad. The lost son, the father who goes all out on a search and rescue, the reunion, the celebration. I'm hardwired to respond lachrymally to that kind of story.

A few years ago I'm on a plane with my eldest daughter. I opt for *Narnia*. Bad move. The bit that really gets me? Greedy Edmund who has betrayed his friends. Stupid, annoying Edmund who caused all the trouble is led into the palace and crowned. Aslan himself declares him to be what not what he was, but what he has become: "Hail Prince Edmund – the just!"

Woah! Here I go! "Dad, you're so embarrassing!"

All those "prodigal son returns" stories hook my heart and squeeze tears out hard, because I know from my own life experience what it is to be really very lost – and then very loved by the real God.

DAD

Let me try another word association with you: GOD.

Your response to that will tell a lot about what you think of him. But I'll try another tack: what did God think about you when you opened your eyes this morning?

Do you think he was ashamed of you? He knows what you have thought, done and said. Was he angry? Is he waiting to judge you? Is he like a Sergeant Major waiting to line you up for inspection? The Bible doesn't just invite, but *commands* that you love the Lord your God with all your heart, mind, soul and strength. But it's hard to love a God like that. You can fear a God like that alright, but LOVE him?

When you stepped into the bathroom and went to look at that man in the mirror, what did God see? A disappointment? Would he prefer you to just go back to bed rather than go and mess up again?

Perhaps he didn't even notice that you woke up. He's got a lot going on in all 125 billion galaxies, with all those planets to spin and stars to count. What's your little life and why should it matter; why should you matter to him? If God is aloof, apathetic, indifferent then it's hard to love a God like that, even if he commands it.

No wonder so many people reject a God like that.

I reject him too, because that's not the real God that I know. I know the one Jesus knows. The *real God*.

When you woke up this morning, the real God had been watching over you every time you rolled over, scratched or snored, with love in his eyes. He never slumbers or sleeps but continually thinks lovingly towards you. The real God loves you unconditionally. He's crazy about you. He doesn't like all you do, because there are consequences to many of those things that break His heart and hurt you and others, but he still thinks you're fantastic. Nothing will change that, because he cannot change.

The real God couldn't wait till you woke up, so you could join in with him in his work in the world. The real God is like the best Dad, but a billion times better, with love a trillion times stronger and more faithful. That's the real God and he's excited to love you!

Here's how one early Jesus-follower described how he felt about his relationship (not his religion, there's a massive difference!) with God.

"How great is the love the Father has lavished on us, that we should be called children of God! And that is what we are!"

Changing how you see God will change how you see yourself. Did you notice that word "lavished"? I love that word! What a picture! You have a heavenly Father who goes OTT, all out, full on. He lays it on thick.

Did you ever think God could be a Dad like that? The real God is. He's put his heart right out there, he leaves nothing unsaid.

What a contrast with so many earthly father / son relationships. B.A. Robertson lyrically described for many the pain of the gap between his ideals for his relationship with his father and the reality. In the song he co-wrote for Mike and the Mechanics, *The Living Years*, he says,

Every generation blames the one before
And all of their frustrations
come beating on your door
I know that I'm a prisoner
to all my father held so dear
I know that I'm a hostage
to all his hopes and fears
I just wish I could have told him
in the living years

No earthly father is perfect, but I was immensely privileged to be the son of Enri Gilmore Delaney. He went to be with his Lord a few years ago now, but I miss him every day. The onset of cancer too soon (it always is) meant there were a few months for late night, long talks and nothing left unsaid between us. The morphine kept him silent for days and I sat with him on his bed as he was dying, playing tapes of his favorite music with no discernable response. I sang along to

Bob Marley's *Three Little Birds*, but the emotion was cracking my voice and it sounded terrible.

"Sorry Dad, not much of a singer."

"I love to hear you sing." His last words to me. Total approval and love.

"Paddy" was the funniest, toughest, kindest man. He worked in various manual jobs to provide for us, though he had one of the finest minds of anyone I have ever met. He laid the love on thick in my life, which helps me understand the real God.

One of my earliest memories was when I was six years of age and Dad was badly burnt all over his body by caustic soda at work. Hospitalized and treated for some time, we couldn't visit the hospital and I missed him terribly. I came home to find him lying on the couch under a thin sheet, sent home to recover. I was told not to touch him, it would hurt him.

So I stood there twitching, shuffling from foot to foot.

He stretched his hand out towards me. There was no way I was going to stand there without getting a hug!

"Come on son, come for your hug."

I knew it hurt him. He did too. I will never, never, never forget lying fully stretched out on his body. My head went on his chest, I listened to his heartbeat and his words of affirmation as he stroked my hair and I knew what it was to be completely loved. Love was defined for me that afternoon. I was just his little boy – I had done nothing to deserve this kind of love, but I was so glad to just soak it all up.

I have told that story in various settings and seen crowds of men cry. So many would do anything (some do kill) for want of love like that from a father. I know how incredibly rare and precious that kind of love is from an earthly dad. I want to love my kids like that.

Whether your earthly dad was awesome, absent or awful, I have good news for you: you can be adopted by a perfect heavenly Father. It has been terribly painful for him, but God has done everything necessary for you to be loved like that, as close as a heartbeat, now and forever. You will only know who you are when you know *whose* you are. He reaches out to you now. He wants you to hear the same words he told your older brother, Jesus, before he ever performed a miracle or preached a sermon, "You are my son, who I love. I am well pleased with you."

Can you imagine how your life could change if you allowed your identity to be transformed by being adopted like that? By the God-Father who throws a party when you return to him? By the one Jesus said you can call by the same name he uses in relating closely to him: "Abba" – Daddy!

> *"How blessed is God! And what a blessing he is! He's the Father of our Master, Jesus Christ, and takes us to the high places of blessing in him. Long before he laid down earth's foundations, he had us in mind, had settled on us as the focus of his love, to be made whole and holy by his love. Long, long ago he decided to adopt us into his family through Jesus Christ."* (Ephesians 1:3 The Message)

Some dear friends of ours just adopted a child. Everything changes. New name, new identity; it's legally binding forever. They are Mum and Dad. They chose to love. The child's job? Be adopted. Receive it. Believe it. Enjoy it.

Who are you? You are who he says you are. Try saying it:

"I am my heavenly Father's son. He loves me. He is well pleased with me."

Really. Say it aloud. Say it till you believe it.

Despite the best efforts of some trendy social engineers,

anyone with their head in the real world knows that dads are irreplaceable in forming a son from boy to man.

There are some things that even the best mother cannot do. No woman, no matter how loving, can be a father. Men need to be around older men to learn the answer to the question of what it really is to be a man or they'll go to all the wrong places and people, make it up and get it wrong. That's why mentoring and cross-generational relationships have to be intentionally put in place. Even the best dads were imperfect; they couldn't teach you all you needed to know.

Example: some dads love to teach their sons about how to fix things practically. My father-in-law came from an engineering background and taught his son how all the tools worked to fix the car or the washing machine. It helped that the son was practical, whereas I'm a klutz.

My dad had a tool box, of course (what man doesn't?), but it was this mysterious, wonderful but incomprehensible treasure trove he would open occasionally. He didn't teach me too much about the contents or how to work them, which may well be the reason I put the Idiot in DIY. He taught me more important lessons like hard work, good humor and how to read before I went to school, so I figured out how to read the Yellow Pages and get someone else to fix the car or washing machine.

THE FATHER'S TOOLBOX

Now I've been adopted by my heavenly Dad, he has lessons to teach me about how to be a man every day. He opens his toolbox to show me how life works and how to fix it when things go wrong. Have a peek with me inside:

Hammer and chisel

Have a look online, search for "The Skit Guys" and their short drama sketch, "God's Chisel". Right after a man prays a simple prayer inviting God to change him, God appears right alongside him with a hammer and chisel. After hilariously establishing the true identity of the visitor, our man submits to the change program, until it hurts. Then control kicks in.

He resists.
Complains.
Justifies.
Points to others worse than him.

Any of that familiar?

I still have a lot of rough edges that need to be knocked off me before God has me ready for his perfection in heaven. Like David, trapped inside a lump of marble needing to be set free by the master sculptor, my Father sees the image of his true Son and wants me to bear the family likeness. He goes to work with the chisel and if pain comes I take it as evidence that he's losing interest, power or love for me – but, in fact, the opposite is true! You may have been subjected to unfair treatment by your earthly father, but your adoptive Dad would never do that.

> *"The LORD disciplines those he loves, as a father the son he delights in."*

But, ouch, the chisel hurts! I don't want that chipped away at, not today anyway!

> *"No discipline seems pleasant at the time, but painful. Later on, however, it produces a harvest of righteousness and peace for those who have been trained by it."* (Hebrews 12:11)

Sandpaper

Sometimes the Father's changes in me are made more gently, rubbed away over time. He knows what he's doing. Remember, he accepts you just as you are, then makes you what only he can help you become. There can be sandpaper situations, sandpaper times, sandpaper people in your life.

The Bible often talks about desert times. We're formed in the wilderness wanderings and what seem like wastelands. When we're disoriented, thirsty and hungry we see what we've been too easily satisfied by and get more desperate for direction and the bread of angels. That's a good place to be.

Why sandpaper? It's a map of the desert! We can't see the way out, but our Father can and he knows that we'll come out from it changed.

A native Indian tribe observes a rite of passage where the boy is taken by his father into the bush, sat on a tree stump and blindfolded. He must now be left alone. He is required to sit there all night. He must obey the father and not remove the blindfold until the rays of the morning sun shine through it. He cannot cry out for help to anyone. Once he survives the night, he is a man. The secrets of this ritual are guarded closely. He cannot tell other boys of this experience, because each lad must come into manhood on his own.

The boy is naturally terrified. He can hear all kinds of noises. Ravenous beasts must surely be surrounding him now. He could be attacked or harmed by man or animal. Wind and leaves play tricks all night, but he must sit wide wake and never remove the blindfold. He must not! This is the only way the boy could become the man!

Finally, after the longest night of his life, the sun appears and the young man removes his blindfold – to discover his father sitting there silently on the stump next to him. He had been at his watch post the entire night, diligently protecting his son. We, too, are never alone. God has promised to never leave or forsake us.

We may not know it or feel like it, but Abba Father is watching over us. In the desert places you learn that just because you can't see or hear God right now, that doesn't mean he is not there. Following the sandpaper map means you walk by faith, not by sight.

Tape measure

On Easter Day this year, a family brought Bert with them to church. He was getting on and not too well – just out from a spell in hospital. I'd met him a few times over the years as he's my best mate's father-in-law: a big, genial, loving guy who'd talk to anyone; the kind of bloke anyone would want as a Granddad. He'd never been to our church before.

In my talk that day I broached the last taboo subject in our society, the only thing you can't talk about in polite conversation: death. We looked at the conclusive evidence that a man had claimed to be able not only to defy, but defeat death because he was God – and then proved the boast. His offer? "There are many mansions in my Father's house. I am going to get one ready for you. Trust me."

One of the illustrations I used was a tape measure – a very long one. I just bought it for the talk and hadn't realized quite how long it was. But I held it up and said that this life that we get so wrapped up in looking after, protecting and worrying about, is just like one tiny inch seen on the tape measure of an eternal perspective. Then I got Alan, who's on staff at my church, to grab the end of the tape measure and he ran way, way back to the doors of the large venue we were using. If I say so myself, it was a pretty good illustration! I said that maybe we need to live our one short life here with more of that eternal reality in mind.

"Are you ready?" I asked people.

Are you ready for what was here long before you got here and will always be there after you?

I invited people to pray, or, if they wanted, me or someone else would pray for them – for healing, for themselves – to respond to the Easter message the way they felt best.

Bert saw Alan walking past, struggled to his feet and asked, "Please, pray like that for me."

Alan could see the man wasn't well. "Do you want me to pray for you to be well? For healing?"

"And the rest. All of that he was saying is on offer, I want all that." They prayed and I believe he received it all.

Two days later I got a call from the family. They took Bert home, then soon after and quite unexpectedly, he really went home. He got the rest.

Moses asked God, "Teach us to number our days aright, that we may gain a heart of wisdom." I join him in that request. You might be successful in many ways in this mortal coil, but before you shuffle off, get wise.

Don't just fix the bike, fix the biker.

I drilled down a little deeper with Noel and heard about a boy, a teen and a man desperate to receive attention, affirmation and unconditional positive regard from that most important of all other men. But instead he received rejection, indifference and disappointment until he stopped going where he knew it wasn't to be found.

I prayed for wisdom and words. This was holy ground. As Jesus once said of another, this man was, "not far from the kingdom of God".

"What if I told you that you could be adopted? Adopted by a perfect Father, who would always be available and would delight to give you all those things?" This was the moment of truth. Now all I could do was await his response and pray. I could hear my heartbeat. The seconds were very long.

A gasp.

Projectile tears came from his eyes. "Yes, oh yes, please. That's what I want, more than anything."

We prayed there and then. He entered the hairpin at speed! Last I heard, Noel was still full throttle or rather riding pillion now, holding tight behind his heavenly Father. Nothing makes me happier.

But there are far too many Noels waiting for adoption.

MY DAD'S BIGGER THAN YOUR DAD (OR MY DAD)

What about you? Ever come to the end of your ability? Good. That's where Abba comes in.

Kids with a loving Dad know what to do. They go to Dad and he opens the tool box and gets to work.

The Father who wants to adopt you has all kinds of tools to help you. You don't know how to make your life work? He specializes in it. He has the power to open up anything that's jammed up. He can easily lift loads that would be impossible for you to carry. He can jump start your dreams, weld together a broken marriage, demolish your enemies, blow away your fears. He can straighten it, level it, build it. Just ask Dad.

Scottish poet and minister George MacDonald commented that "... the refusal to look up to God as our father is the one central wrong in the whole human affair; the inability, the one central misery."

Can I get technical? MacDonald went on to explain that the word that most Bibles translate as "adoption" goes far beyond our understanding that someone who was an outsider becomes a son. The word could be translated, "taken to be a son".

MacDonald says it "... does not imply that God adopts children that are not his own, but rather that a second time he fathers his own; that a second time they are born – this time from above; that he will make himself tenfold, yea, a hundredfold, their father. He will have them into the very bosom wherefore they issued ... He will have them one with himself. It was for the sake of this that, in his Son, he died for them."

You don't have to understand all of that to know it. I'll sum it up in four words personally addressed to you from the real God, the perfect Father who will take you as a son:

"Come for your hug."

Father
Fitness
Friends
JESUS
Finances
Family
Failures

"I am an historian, I am not a believer, but I must confess as a historian that this penniless preacher from Nazareth is irrevocably the very centre of history. Jesus Christ is easily the most dominant figure in all history."

—H.G. Wells

EIGHT

Jesus

[the ultimate Diamond Geezer]

TEA TIME

He was in his early forties when the voice started. An inner voice appeared, as indistinct as a whisper at first, but becoming louder and more insistent:

"There's more to life."

He looked in the mirror one morning and it wasn't the love handles or the extra silver shooting through his mane that alarmed him. The years just seemed to be flying faster and he'd subtly began to question what it was really all about.

"There's more to life."

11.10am, shine right shoe on hallway carpet, head towards lift.

It was a small town and he was a larger than life guy. Everyone knew Zac. He'd made his money the hard way through property and loans. Some called him a shark, but that's what made him a big fish. He had more than enough money now, though he could always use a little more, since his earnings could never quite match his yearnings. He adjusted the diamond tiepin.

11.13am, press button, satisfying ping.

Business travel and extra leisure time he'd once enjoyed now provided unwanted periods to ponder, wrestle with and push away the nagging thoughts about what others would call success – as opposed to significance. He had the pounds, but what about purpose? What had he ever done that really counted? Who knew him beyond the externals?

He could be funny and sharp-witted. The guys he did business with laughed along. Everyone knew Zac could always be relied upon to give forth with a whisky in hand. But how many of them really gave a damn?

He shook off such thoughts. Focus!

He checked his Rolex Yachtmaster, which of course kept perfect time, but that wasn't his source of pride. No, you could say what you wanted about Z. P. Goldstein (people said many things, only some of which were untrue) but you could never say he was late.

Or early.

Just on time. Exactly on time. Punctual.

Everyone knew that the lift doors would open and he would step into the reception area at 11.14am. His mother had instilled into him this value, the mark of a true gentleman. "His timing was impeccable." It said everything about a man. Timing was everything. It was something he was fastidious about. Punctuality – spelt OCD.

People could set their watches by him – the cleaners, the reception staff, the baggage clerks. He straightened starched cuffs and readied himself to go out and meet his public. The lift doors opened and he walked through the lobby of his hotel.

His. All his.

The luxuriant carpets were his, the opulent mahogany-clad reception area, his. Onyx statues and the marble busts. His.

The staff were his.

His staff. They smiled widely as they greeted him passing by, though more than once in the highly polished interiors he'd glimpsed a pale reflection of their faces changing as they thought he could not see them. He knew they complained about the wages and he'd sacked a few old timers, but what was a man to do in such hard times?

The sun momentarily scorched the top of his balding head as he tried to cover the patch and pat it down with his embroidered handkerchief. He cursed himself for forgetting his hat, but it shouldn't matter, except his car was seconds late! His doorman appeared Mephisto-like at his side, opening a sunshade with a flourish as he waited for the Limo to appear. Now the door had opened and he disappeared into the dark, cool interior.

11.15am.

He'd made it.

But what have I made? "There's more ..."

The driver – he could never remember their names – turned the music low to apologize and mumble some lame excuse about bad traffic as Zac received his Martini. He was going to his racecourse, where he would see his horse win the 11.30 race. It would win because it was lighter than all the other horses. The adjudicators and officials were his. He would present the trophy himself standing with his jockey later, and the cameras would flash for the sports pages as he dripped sweat without a hat, but nobody would comment. At least, not out loud. Some would sneer at a distance as others cursed, screwing up their losing slips in disgust. If people didn't like him winning they shouldn't play the game.

The blonde in the back of the car pouring, putting olives in his drink, told him how nice he looked today. He knew she was paid to flatter, but received the compliment without a sound and adjusted his tie. Some said they wanted to mother him. He was more than happy to let them for a while, until he got what he wanted and moved on. Why could he never remember their names?

11.17am. The car stopped.

11.19am. The car stayed stopped. What's going on?

"Sorry sir, traffic seems snarled up. I'll try to find a way round it."

No way. Going nowhere, fast or slow. They were stuck in the middle of a vast crowd that had overflowed onto the road. No one could see in through the tinted windows, but they all knew his car anyway. Some gestured rudely as the driver honked the horn louder and more insistently. He barked obscenities at nobody in particular.

11.22am. "GET OUT AND SEE WHAT THE HOLD UP IS!"

"Yessir! Right away Sir!"

11.25am. This was intolerable in his town. Where has that driver got to? Why am I paying the clown? What's the hold up? At this rate ...

No!

He would not permit the thought, but he couldn't push down the nauseating, dawning reality. Time waits for no man. Not even him.

At this rate, he would be … late!

He would not pull through the gates in time. The limo would not park in his private space in time. Because he was LATE. Those assigned to clear the way through the crowd to his enclosure would pat their timepieces in disbelief. Could it be?

It could not be. The thought was intolerable.

At times, he'd been snubbed by those who considered themselves respectable or religious because of how he'd made, not inherited, his wealth. He could live with that. On other occasions he'd seen those who he'd had muscled out of their (no, his!) houses spit in the street as he'd walked by. He could live with that. His own family might not like him, his wife might have left him, all of them calling him greedy and a liar on their way out – none of them could live long with him – but he could live with that.

But he would not, could not, live with being late! He looked at the watch again, but despite its extortionate price tag, it could not bring him the joy it promised, because he was now, officially, running late.

He made a decision. Pulled the catch back. Outside it was sweltering. The crowd was still there, in fact it seemed to have grown. He had to push hard on the door with his shoulder to make room to step out. So was this what the worst day of Zaccheaus P Goldstein's life would feel like?

There was only one thing he hated more than being late. Crowds. He hated crowds. In fact, he arranged his life to avoid crowds. On school photographs he'd always been at the front, never the back row. His parents were beanstalks and said he'd grow taller soon enough ... but the promised growth spurt never came. The name-calling began early. The other kids soon learned that what he lacked in size he made up for in fury when you crossed him. The girls knew not to wear heels on the red carpet with him and not get caught alongside him on camera. He preferred to walk alone.

But in a crowd he always felt alone. And small. The smallest adult, and even the kids these days were beanstalks!

He braced himself for stares and sniggers. Was that the worst they could do? Bring it on!

A shiny size-four shoe stepped out, metal segs to give an extra inch always made a sharp clicking sound, distinctly heard over the noise of the crowd. What noise?

No noise.

That's what was different about this crowd. Silence. A strained silence, like when everyone's trying to hear.

"Hey! What's going on? What's the hold up? Get out of ..."

Hundreds of eyes looked down at him, stripped him of power with their disdain. They didn't even have to say, "Shh!"

It was silent again.

No. Not silence. There was a voice. That's what everyone was trying to hear!

Carried on the warm breeze, wafting over the infuriatingly stupid beanstalks that surrounded him. What was that voice? And what was it saying? Muffled, indistinct ... snatches of tantalizing promise.

"I have come, that you might have life."

Somehow familiar? He needed to see the source. He hated this crowd more than any other. How could he make a way?

"I am the way...
I am the truth
I am the life...
If anyone comes to me, I will never turn him away..."

A poet? Seriously, are all these people stopping just to listen to a poet?

"It's easier for a camel to pass through the eye of a needle...
(laughter from the crowd)
than for a rich man to enter the kingdom of heaven..."

Is he talking about me? Who is that?

The voice didn't seem accusing, just somehow sad. But heads swiveled and eyes turned to look down at him again – hating, accusing, jealous – but then the worst look of them all? Pity.

It didn't matter that he was now late. The power in these words spoke to that other voice inside him. It seemed even to be the same voice. Nobody ever spoke like this man!

The voice grew louder, perhaps twenty feet away, but he couldn't see. Zac pictured himself as a tiny flower being crowded out by worthless weeds. Anger started to flare, but now the voice he'd heard inside and the voice in the street spoke in tune:

"A man's life does not consist of the abundance of his possessions..."

No! The voice was getting quieter! He tried to push through, but the crowd closed ranks, suffocating.

"The thief comes to steal, kill and destroy - but I have come so you may have life in all its fullness!"

"Truly I say to you ... unless .... man...
he cannot ...
.... the kingdom of God."

What? Unless a man what ?

There was only one thing to do. It didn't matter what anyone thought, he had to hear the speaker. Had to see the face behind the words that were challenging, convicting, calling. He put his hands on the hot roof, a foot in the doorway, and clambered on top of the limousine. It somehow didn't matter that the suit was creasing or the segs scratching the roof. He had to hear! He had to see!

Spinning himself around he tried to orient himself to where the voice had last come from. He looked to the front of the car and came face to face … with the voice.

He would tell about this first impression many times and in many other places.

This guy isn't much taller than me. Workman's clothes. Surrounded by a gang, obviously his friends, all dressed like the guys who work at my factory. Ordinary? No way. Authority. He exudes it, no, it emanates from him in a way designer clothes, jewels and all the trappings of wealth can only promise but never really deliver. Power like a President and something incredibly, well, *good* about him. All around him, an aura, a fragrance no perfumer could reproduce. Purity, like seeing a young bride on her wedding day.

We lock eyes and I immediately want to pull mine away, but I can't. He still hasn't spoken and for the first time in my life, it stops.

Time.

Time stops. There's a heaviness in the air that has nothing to do with the heat of the day. I want to hold my breath.

Because it's like time doesn't exist around this man, like he carries eternity round with him.

"Zacchaeus..."

He knows me.

He knows my name.

He knows all about me.

For the first time in my life, something else happens. I wish I wasn't standing tall in a crowd.

I'm wishing he hadn't noticed me. Why did I stand up on this stupid car? Why couldn't I have stayed low in the crowd and listened to the words and let him pass? Because now everyone's looking at me. But worse than that, he's looking at me with those eyes. Like he knows.

He knows my name. He knows it all. Every shady deal done on the side. Every bribe taken or given. Everyone I ever hurt to gain everything I own. And surely now he knows the truth he must denounce me. It's dirty laundry time. Another voice inside accuses me, "Zacchaeus! You lying, cheating, selfish thief! Get down! You don't deserve to be here." I know that's what I should hear. It's what I have sometimes said to myself when lying alone at night, or when lying to someone else. The truth about me that everyone in the crowd knows, is that I am a real sinner, and they don't even know the half of it. But then I realize, that's not his voice. He's not talking at all. Just smiling.

Now he opens his mouth, smiles more broadly, and says, "I don't have a watch. What time is it?"

I don't even have to look at mine. The internal clock says, "11.45am."

"You mean tea time! I'm coming to your place!"

SHORT CHANGED

My retelling of the historical events described by Dr Luke in his gospel can't begin to convey the sense of shock that the crowd must have felt the day a respectable, popular Rabbi named Jesus of Nazareth entered a town called Jericho and bypassed the religious leaders to invite himself as a guest at the home of a notorious tax collector called Zaccheaus.

> "Jesus is the God whom we can approach without pride and before whom we can humble ourselves without despair."
>
> —Blaise Pascal

Jesus had included a tax collector called Levi among his closest followers, which must have raised some eyebrows. Tax collectors were known collaborators with the hated Roman conquerors, impure because they handled their money and took some of it for themselves.

Zaccheaus was a *chief* tax collector, for which we can read "universally despised".

The Jewish people placed great value on meals and hospitality, it was much more than just eating. If I shared a meal with you I was showing you acceptance. I was saying, "I am willing to share my life with you." This is one reason why a Jew would not enter the home of a Gentile in those days.

If you have ever been to Sunday school this story will be familiar to you because it's an easy one for the teachers to get the kids to reenact. You always get the shortest kid to play Zaccheaus, of course. That's because it says he, *"... wanted to see who Jesus was but he could not because of the crowd, for he was a short man."*

One of the few interesting things I learned at theological college was that in the original Greek text it's not exactly clear who the short man of the two was. It just says Zac couldn't see Jesus because he was small. Who? Who was small? Jesus or Zaccheaus?

It could have been Zaccheaus, so I stuck with that traditional thought rather than annoy too many people. But the way my Bible tells it, Jesus of Nazareth was just as much God-come-among-us to bring heaven to earth if he was six foot four and full of muscles or a baby in a manger. When I've shared that thought at men's meetings it usually elicits at least one cheer – from the little guy at the back of the room!

Coal men are all about appearance, but God sees the reality. That's what Zaccheaus discovered the day Jesus came to his house. I have talked about that little guy often in men's meetings because I think he has so many lessons to teach us blokes.

Why did he climb a sycamore tree when Jesus was passing by? Perhaps it was so he could have the upper hand. He's up here, Jesus is down there. He's got God right where he wants him. He's not anti-God, he knows where he is if he needs him. Lots of blokes I know are most comfortable keeping God at arms length like that.

Jesus is having none of it.

He says, "I want to come to your house – today."

What do you do with that?

What if he's talking to you?

He knows your name.

He knows all about you.

What would change if Jesus came to your house?

You might think he comes to condemn, to judge, to blame. He could. He knows you, fellah. He would be totally justified and if you disagree it's only because you're self-deceived and can add pride to the list. But that's not what he came for. Jesus described his mission succinctly as he dabbed his lips on a fine napkin after the meal at Zacchaeus' place: "I have come to seek and save the lost."

I don't think that rich man woke up that day feeling lost, but he was. We men are not good at asking for directions, and we are certainly not going to admit to being lost are we? It's even worse when you're married, when your wife (who you know is geographically challenged by virtue of being the weaker sex) says, "We passed the sign way back there ..."

What do men do? We celebrate our manhood by keeping on going. Carry on regardless.

Because we want the wrong road to become the right road.

Sometimes, no matter how hard you want that to happen, the wrong road just keeps getting longer and wronger. You have to change something. You have to ask for directions.

Eventually, you have to do the hardest thing for a man to do. Get off the road at a petrol station or something, turn around, and go the other way. And the Bible has a word for that. Repentance. It literally means, "Change your mind."

Zacchaeus had tried to give the impression that he was a Diamond Geezer, but on close inspection the flaws were all too apparent. The great news in the story is that Jesus knew all that and accepted him. He loved him as he was. Jesus went home with him, insisted on it – even though he wasn't religious or even a very good person (both of which make having Jesus at home very hard indeed).

Everyone said, "How come he's going to be the guest of a notorious sinner?" But Zaccheaus wasn't listening to the crowd now. They got home and the friendship developed, and it seems the chief tax collector really did recognize that he was in truly exalted company as he said, "Look, Lord, I'm going to give away half of everything I have to the poor. And if I've defrauded anyone, I'll pay it back fourfold!" (If?!)

I don't think Jesus told him to do that. This was the start of the process of a coal man being formed into a true Diamond Geezer – a man with nothing to prove and nothing to hide; a man who could be tough, transparent and trusted. Because he now knew he was treasured!

Jesus didn't come to his house to pore over the accounts, but to pour the teapot (they were both Englishmen of course!) There was something about being befriended, loved and welcomed by the Son of God that made all that other stuff seem so much less valuable in comparison. He was changed from the inside out.

Then, Zac went to work on his *finances*. Who knows, maybe the next thing would be his *fitness* and he signed up for the Jericho 10k? Perhaps he got back in touch with some of his *family* to apologize and attempt to rebuild those relationships? Having Jesus as his *friend* and seeing how close Jesus was with his disciples, wouldn't he want to learn how to be a better friend now? I don't know what happened next, but I know the change happens not from us trying harder (been there, not done that). We might try to change the outside, but the way God works is from the inside out.

INSIDE JOB

Centuries before Jesus walked into that town, another bloke who others thought too small to take on giant tasks had a surprising God-encounter. A prophet called Samuel comes to a village called Bethlehem (before it or any of its inhabitants were famous) to select the new king of Israel from the sons of a man called Jesse.

They're lined up in height order. Any man who was never picked for the footie team knows what it is to be in that line. The youngest boy, who the siblings are jealous of and the father dismissive of, isn't even *at* the party. He's away doing a servant's job, looking after the sheep. Samuel and his Jesse agree the oldest son looks the part. But God rejects them all one by one:

> *"Do not look on his appearance or on the height of his stature, because I have rejected him. For the Lord sees not as man sees: man looks on the outward appearance, but the Lord looks on the heart."*

This is a word for us, men. "The Lord sees not as man sees." Do you see that yet? He saw David's heart, the heart of a Diamond Geezer. How does he you see you? How do you see yourself?

UP CLOSE AND PERSONAL

Well done for reading this far. Most men don't read anything except the paper or anything they are made to read for work.

I commend and thank you. There are a lot less pages at this end of the book and I hope for some of you decision-time approaches, not only about the external changes you might want to make to the outside of the Diamond. It's the inside that matters to God. Wherever you picked this book up, Christianity should never appear in the self-help section.

I want to start to get close and personal like Jesus did with the little coal man of Jericho now. What's your next step after reading the book? I hope, if nothing else, what I've written gives you the appetite to go and get a Bible. Start with, say, Mark's gospel. It's the shortest and rather than rely on what anyone else might have told you about that most amazing of all books, actually read it for yourself.

Check out the stories and accounts I've only had chance to allude to. Maybe you can imagine yourself in the story as these historical events took place, observing the action (that's what I did to write the story at the start of this chapter). This invitation comes with a spiritual health warning, however. Be prepared for Jesus Christ to walk off the pages and show you that he knows you too, as he's done for countless millions before you.

IT HAPPENED TO ME

At Primary school I was told the stories of Jesus. I probably heard Zaccheaus' story in some assembly or religious study class. Perhaps it was even mentioned in the obligatory hours in chapel which convinced me there was such a place as purgatory. I heard that Jesus was the Son of God, that he had died for the sins of the world. I didn't know what any of that meant and so it meant nothing.

When I was thirteen I decided to "give God a go" – to see if he was there, hoping he wasn't so I could get on with life without him. I endured services for almost every day in Lent, and though there were various liturgical prayers being intoned I said only one: "If there's anybody up there you'd better show me you're real. Show me, or I'm out of here."

Nothing.

Good. If there was no God I could live however I wanted (I'd figured out the natural consequences of atheism pretty early).

At the end of school I visited the careers advisor at school and told her I wanted to join either the Army or the Police. She asked what my parents did. "They work in a mill."

"You should work in the mill."

"I don't want to work in the mill."

"What does your older brother do?" she asked.

"He works in the same mill." (Terry's summer job there has now lasted over thirty years).

"You should work in the mill."

"I don't want to work in the mill."

"What's wrong with working in the mill?"

"Nothing, I just want to join the Police."

"No chance, you're too small!"

"I'm only sixteen, I think I might grow. Anyway, I've heard they have Police Cadets. I wonder if you have any information on that?"

"No, but I can help you apply to work in the mill."

At sixteen I told my parents I was going to college. I went out one morning, then played table tennis and then went to my Italian friend and boxing training partner Pete's house to drink his dad's home made wine all afternoon. That lasted about a month with nobody knowing except me and Pete. I think Pete's dad started to guess though, because he began to hide the *vino tinto*. I decided I really had to get a job, so I applied for the Police Cadets.

I went for the test for the Police and passed the written examinations. There were some medicals. I remember, having done the eyesight test, the optician said, "You have sniper vision." I was downcast. Some stupid problem with my eyes was going to keep me out of the Police? He explained that it wasn't a bad thing, but a good thing, then asked me if I'd taken the intelligence test yet.

A few days later I went for the interview for the Police Cadets. There was a panel of three, with a dour Scottish Inspector the only one who spoke. "It says on your CV you like doing magic card tricks?" I did then, it was an interest, the kind of thing your mum says is a waste of time because you'll never get a job doing that.

He opened a draw in his desk. "Amaze me."

I did a fairly rubbish trick and got the job. Mum's not always right.

I bumped into the careers woman a week later and when I told her she was delighted. "I've never got anyone into the Police Cadets before!"

The Cadets bore little relation to the real Police it turned out, but was brilliant in its own way. In two years I got super fit, learning Judo and Aikido. I also discovered canoeing, climbing and carnal knowledge.

One quiet evening on security duty, walking round the Training College, I saw a poster on the wall that some religious nutter had put up: "Christian Police Association Meeting, Thursday, 7.00pm." Some voice inside that sounded like my own said, "You should go to that."

"Na! No way!" I carried on. But even now I could take you to the exact spot where the poster was.

Jesus is the ultimate "fisher of men" and it was like God had a hook in my heart. But I pulled away on the line and wasn't going to come easily.

At eighteen and a half years of age I was a Police Officer walking the beat in Cheetham Hill, Manchester, one of the toughest beats in the UK. The officer who showed me the ropes also showed me that although I thought I could drink, I was way behind him. The depiction in the TV drama *Life On Mars* was close but somewhat understated. The force was unbelievable in terms of drinking, womanizing and violence. I lived for all three.

Then the miner's strike erupted and I became one of the bad guys in Billy Elliot. Scary, hairy times. I was at what became known as The Battle of Orgreave, on the day Arthur Scargill was arrested. Mum had told me to keep my head down. I was two rows back from the front line. I thought I was safe, until the coke trucks driven by working miners came into view. Suddenly, thousands of big angry miners were pushing thousands of their "enemy" policemen and the force of the two buckled against one another. I found myself pushed up on the crest of a human wave, unable to breath or move at all, as delighted miners began to throw bricks and sticks at my extremely pale head.

I think after the miner's strike I lost it for a few years. I don't want to go into too much detail, and I'm not proud of this. There are some things I did that I don't even want to try to remember, but I was definitely in slow self-destruct mode.

I hurt some good people. Too many women, some of whom were happy to just have sex, but some who wanted a relationship I was not interested in. I also enjoyed hurting bad people. I found I was quite good at violence as I got bigger and working where I was gave me good opportunity to learn how to get better at it.

One day I turned a corner to see a lad my age trying to nick a car. I chased him a while until he suddenly stopped running. He figured he could take me in a fight and we had a long time finding out. Only at the Police Station did I discover he was one of the infamous Noonan brothers who went on to achieve legendary status as Manchester's gangster baddies.

The drinking was getting worse and worse. I had my own flat at twenty, a place where I was utterly unaccountable. I sometimes went to work as a Police Officer with a mouthful of extra strong mints to hide the smell of drink.

I was badly beaten up by a gang one night as I came out of a nightclub. A soccer hooligan I was at school with pointed me out as an off-duty copper and I found myself surrounded, nose broken and on the floor for a good kicking. It was the worst beating of my life, but we did manage to bring most of them to justice later.

Around that time a nurse called Zoe heard about this wild and out-of-control policeman. She was engaged to a fireman I knew. 999. When she first saw me she didn't like what she saw. I still remember seeing her and thinking, "Tasty, but too posh."

It was New Years Eve, at some night club. I'd had more than a few, but had developed a high tolerance. I saw a lovely girl dancing. As midnight struck I put myself in front of her for a kiss and it happened. A great kiss – one of the three greatest in history – spoilt only by her fiancé who took a swing at me. Within minutes we were both thrown out by the bouncers. I know it's not your usual, "How the church minister met his wife" story.

A few weeks later Zoe broke up their relationship. Nothing to do with me – she had made a commitment to follow Jesus Christ a few years before and realized that her life wasn't lining up with that. It was him or God, so he went.

I tried to move in. No way. She only wanted a friend.

I'll be your friend.

Eventually, I got her to go to the pictures with me "as a friend". Great film. A classic. Arnold Schwarzenegger in

Commando. She didn't like it. Good job it was "cheap night". But there was something different about this one. Something shone from her – a Diamond Girly – but I was a coal man through and through. She said we could be friends, but she wouldn't be interested in any further relationship because I wasn't a Christian. I told her I was, that it's a Christian country. "No," she said, "the Hindus and Muslims would disagree."

So I tried to put her off God and get her into me. I asked her all those tough questions like, "How did Noah get all those animals on the ark?" and "What did they do for forty days and forty nights?"

"I suppose they went fishing."

"They couldn't do much with only two worms."

I told her about some of the terrible things I'd seen. "How can there be a good God when that happens?" I wasn't interested in the answer. I just knew it was a good one to get God-botherers squirming.

She didn't try to convert me, which was infuriating.

One day she said, "You keep asking these questions. If you really want to know what I believe, there's a man coming speaking at a church next week. I have to be at that to help with the kids work. If you want you can come with me?"

That sounded like a date!

"Only if I can take you to the pub after?" I'd even put up with a bit of church for that.

"Okay."

I went into the church building and was amazed to see it full. Full of smiling people who actually looked normal and like they wanted to be there. The music was actually good too – in church!

Then there was a drama – in church!

Acted by young people – in church!

I only remember the end. A guy in a white T-shirt, who I figured was Jesus, saying he was the light of the world. But then he was dragged up a stepladder and they stretched out his arms wide and mimed hammering nails in as someone read some words which I later found came straight from the Bible:

"This is the verdict: Light has come into the world, but men loved darkness instead of light because their deeds were evil. Everyone who does evil hates the light, and will not come into the light for fear that his deeds will be exposed."

Well that was me. But I wasn't ready to admit that right then. In fact, if you'd asked, I considered myself to be a good person. You could probably have found any number of ex-girlfriends who'd disagree, but after all I was a Police Officer, shiny buttons on my uniform, shiny teeth, shiny boots. If I ever felt bad about my own track record I could always arrest another baddy to compare myself with so I would feel better.

After the drama, a guy got up to speak. Oh good. He would be boring and irrelevant. Wrong again. Eric Delve is one of finest, most passionate, gifted orators the Church in England has ever produced. He produced a nail, held it aloft. "This is a roman nail, dug up near Hadrian's Wall. 2000 years old. This is the kind of nail Jesus would have had driven into him ..." Then with fire in his eyes he went on to describe how the cross was not just a story but *history*. It was not an example of what happens when a good man gets a raw deal, but this was the Son of God, whipped, stripped, beaten beyond recognition and abandoned by those closest to him.

He graphically described how at Calvary Jesus Christ bore our sins, became our sins. Jesus the Son of God became the sin of Adam, of every man who had ever lived and broke the laws of God. The only innocent one bore the punishment, so we guilty ones could be acquitted. He had said that he would die as a ransom for many and rise again from the dead to prove his claims, and then he did!

Well that was pretty good I thought. Good speaker. Let's get to the pub.

A few evenings later I went to the meeting again, on the same condition – that it was a prelude to the pub.

At the end they offered some free literature if anyone was interested. Well, I found it interesting, did that count? I decided I might try church one Sunday. I went to the front as the band played something majestic and got my free books. Zoe's mum hugged me and seemed very excited, but I took the books home unread and put them in my sock drawer.

A few days later Zoe had a present for me. Things were definitely looking up. I opened it. But it was a Bible. That was very weird, but I said I liked it. I told her I was definitely a Christian. She didn't buy it.

Then I opened it. She'd written inside:

To Anthony
Mark 8:34
Love Zoe

Love?

She put love there! Get in!

The stuff in the middle must be a code. The ex-fiancé was called Mark. Was this about him? No. It must be in the Bible, stupid. She helped me find the gospel of Mark. I was thinking this verse might say, "Okay, because I think you are good looking and funny, I will go out with you." It didn't say that.

It said, *"If any man would come after me, he must deny himself, and take up his cross, and follow me."*

Follow who?

What cross? Jesus had a cross. Who else needed a cross?

"I don't know what this means."

"You're not a Christian."

Poo.

I really liked this girl! I decided to go to church with her a bit, maybe that would fool her.

> **"God may thunder his commands from Mount Sinai and men may fear, yet remain at heart exactly as they were before. But let a man once see his God down in the arena as a man – suffering, tempted, sweating and agonized, finally dying a criminal's death – and he is a hard man indeed who is untouched."**
>
> —J.B. Phillips, *Your God Is Too Small*

A few weeks later, I was driving to work in a mini (the car, not a skirt, I wasn't undercover or anything). Someone from her church had lent me a tape with some of the more modern kind of songs they were using, so I put it on. It was just background music on the road through an awful part of the city called Gorton. One song came on. It was called, *The Servant King*.

Hands that flung stars into space
To cruel nails surrendered

What was that? Wind it back. (You could do that easily with tapes!)

Hands that flung stars into space
To cruel nails surrendered

Wham! What follows next might freak you out. It did me. For good. Forever.

The presence of God invaded the car. That is the ONLY way I can describe it. Somehow, I pulled over to the side of the road as I had a full on, Technicolor, 3D vision of Jesus on the cross. Blood and guts. Such courage. I knew that Jesus was the toughest man who ever lived, because of what I saw in that vision. I also knew he was the Son of God, because he was alive and he was coming closer to me.

Oh no.

He is God.

He knows. About me.

He knows it all. What nobody else knows. What nobody should ever know.

He has seen it all, heard it all. He IS the Truth and he knows the truth.

I felt like I was covered in excrement as this incredible holiness drew closer. I didn't even know the Ten Commandments, but I knew I must have broken them all. I wanted to die. I deserved to die. I wanted to hide, but it's hard to hide from God – especially in a mini.

I had been in court many times as a witness. There is an authority about such places. I loved to see the guilty punished. But what about me? Magnify the awe of a human courtroom immeasurably as I began to despair at the thought that Jesus is God and he could and should and must judge me. But just then ...

Grace.

Love.

Mercy

Grace, grace, grace upon grace.

"You are loved. I love you, son. I forgive you. I have a plan for you. Follow me. Mercy. Grace. Love. Love. Let me in. Grace."

I knew from a boy that "Jesus died for the sins of the whole world." I just didn't know that meant me.

"Let me in your life. "

Now, it was personal. He had done everything for me.

"Yes, Lord." That was all it took and all I wanted to say. I said it.

I hadn't cried since being a little boy, except those times watching *Shenandoah* on Saturday afternoons. You'd have had to hit me very hard to make me cry. God didn't even lay a finger on me. But I cried alright.

And then I was late for work.

The sergeant asked why. "I'm a Christian, Sarge."

"Well you're not a very good one. You're late!"

I rang Zoe and told her. She believed me. She believed it had really happened to me.

THE ADVENTURE OF FAITH

Since then, I have never had a boring day. I've had a few tedious minutes, a lot of mundane hours, I'll grant you. But from the day I yielded myself to follow God's plan for my life right up to now, it has been an adventure. I stayed in the Police for another eight years and loved serving God there. During that time he called me to train as a minister – a long story for another time – and he has transformed me from someone afraid to even speak a prayer out loud in a room of ten people, to someone who has been privileged to speak to thousands and (on the radio) even millions.

Following God's plan was far better, bigger and bolder than any I could have dreamt up for myself.

I have only ever loved one woman and I'm committed to enjoying loving her for the rest of my life. My children love and serve God. I have witnessed miracles of healing, provision and life change. He's taken me with him to various nations around the world including India after the tsunami and Haiti right after the earthquake, to be his hands and feet to help others. Now he has brought me back to the city I grew up in to be part of his work here again with a great church family, not serving the law, but sharing grace.

It's my conviction, looking back, that God was always watching over my life, even before that climactic moment of decision. He was more obviously there when I stood at that poster, and less so in church as a child; but he was always there. Many biblical characters came to the same staggering conclusion. King David looked back over a remarkable life and traced the hand of God even back to the time when, *"You created my inmost being; you knit me together in my mother's womb ... your eyes saw my unformed body. All the days ordained for me were written in your book before one of them came to be."*

"The secular response to the Christ story always goes like this: he was a great prophet, obviously a very interesting guy, had a lot to say along the lines of other great prophets, be they Elijah, Muhammad, Buddha or Confucius. But actually Christ doesn't allow you that. He doesn't let you off that hook. Christ says, 'No. I'm not saying I'm a teacher, don't call me teacher. I'm not saying I'm a prophet. I'm saying: "I'm the Messiah." I'm saying, "I am God incarnate." And people say: "No, no, please, just be a prophet. A prophet, we can take." ... Christ took on the sins of the world so that what we put out did not come back to us, and .... our sinful nature does not reap the obvious death. That's the point. It should keep us humbled. It's not our own good works that get us through the gates of heaven."

—Bono (Bono In Conversation With Michka Assayas)

I read what the apostle Paul wrote two thousand years ago to an early group of Christ-followers in a place called Ephesus and find the three-part story of God's work in their lives mirrors my own exactly: *Wow, how* and *now.*

WOW:

"As for you, you were **dead** *in your transgressions and sins, in which you used to live."*

Until I met Jesus, I wasn't bad and needing to get better, I was dead and needing resurrection. Wow! I had no power to help or change myself in any real or lasting way. When he showed me his greatness and power, I finally saw how much I needed outside intervention to accomplish internal transformation. That's the bad news. You need to know how bad the bad news is before you will gladly welcome the good news.

HOW:

"...it is by grace you have been saved, through faith—and this not from yourselves, it is the gift of God— not by works, so that no one can boast."

As part of basic training in the Police I had to become qualified as a lifeguard. One of the first things you learn is that you can't save someone who's trying to save themselves. For the first twenty-one years of my life, his grace was on offer but it was a gift I didn't think I needed any more than a flower offered by a Hare Krishna at the airport. When I was ready, and stopped trying to be good enough, he showed me that what Jesus had done already made me acceptable. That's how it has to happen, by grace.

NOW:

"For we are God's workmanship, created in Christ Jesus to do good works, which God prepared in advance for us to do."

Too often Christians stop at the second stage. We ask for forgiveness from Jesus as a kind of "get out of hell free" card, and then pretty much live for ourselves and depend on ourselves. But grace is far more than what God gives us one day so he doesn't have to punish us for our sins. Gordon Fee described grace as, "the empowering presence of God, enabling me to be all God calls me to be and do all God calls me to do."

I recently heard John Ortberg describe grace as, "God doing in me, what I could not do myself – and have not earned." That means we are not supposed to just be saved by grace, but to LIVE by grace! Now, every day. You are your heavenly Father's workmanship, His favorite project is to change us from coal men to Diamond Geezers, who look, think and act like his Son – because he has laid out before you now a destiny, a great purpose, a difference to make today – and his grace enables it to become a reality.

MAN IN THE MIRROR

A man checks into a run-down hotel and is asked, "Do you have a good memory for faces?"

"Yes I do."

"Good, you'll need it when you shave because there's no mirror in your room."

Did you know Jesus had younger brothers and sisters? How hard would that have been? How many times do you think they were told off with, "Why can't you be like your older brother?" The siblings didn't believe that Jesus really was the Son of God. Familiarity breeds contempt. One of the brothers was called James and he didn't believe right up until after he saw Jesus die on the cross. He was only transformed when Jesus, his half -brother, burst open the tombstone and reappeared alive again before him.

Actually, a case could be made that none of the disciples were really followers of Jesus as the Son of God until after the resurrection. They were followers of Jesus the remarkable but human Rabbi of Nazareth, trying to pattern their lives around his teaching and example. It's possible to do that, to have Jesus as your life coach and have many of the principles of wisdom work in your life, but that's not why he came because that's not all he is.

Within a few decades of becoming a fully convinced follower of Jesus Christ, James wrote a very practical instructional note to other believers, wherein he says the teaching of the Bible is like a mirror.

"Act on what you hear! Those who hear and don't act are like those who glance in the mirror, walk away, and two minutes later have no idea who they are, what they look like."

He said it's possible to be deceived, even to deceive ourselves. You can come to the end of a book like this and think the fact that you've actually finished it helps. No. Don't kid yourself. Unless you do something, it's useless. What do you do?

You have to *Explore* the concepts. Go back through the book. What jumped out at you? What made you think in each of the different sections?

Examine yourself, your current reality. If you were pushed in one of these facets – family, father, friendships etc. – which one would you crumble in? Where do you shine?

Establish a plan. What changes do you need to make? The principles outlined will work for anyone, whether you believe in Jesus Christ or not, but it would be a tragedy if, for example, you got fitter physically but didn't grow spiritually, or straightened out your finances at the cost of your soul.

You have to *Engage* creatively and seek to apply what you're being shown. Maybe you're not ready yet to become a Christ-follower, but even if you believe that a fraction of what I have said is true, you're at the brink of making the most important decision of your life.

THE ONLY PERFECT MAN

What I've tried to do in my own imperfect way is hold up a Diamond to you, a perfect, absolutely *flawless* Diamond. The only perfect man.

Have you seen yourself in the mirror? Do you have an accurate picture?

Do you have the real picture of who Jesus Christ really is? Remember what A W Tozer wrote,

"What comes into our minds when we think about God is the most important thing about us."

That stained glass portrayal of a pale, thin, bearded man in a nightie with a shiny plate around his head has put more men off than almost anything else. I don't think Jesus ever looked like that – and I know for a fact that he doesn't look like that now, because I've read the end of the story – the book of Revelation. When the real Jesus showed up at the end of the Bible to a man who had known him as a friend, the awesome power he radiated caused John to fall to the ground like a dead man.

The real Jesus depicted in the Bible is no longer, "gentle Jesus, meek and mild" (he's been there and done that). He is a warrior! His face shines brighter than the noonday sun. Resplendent, all-powerful, arms like rods of crysolite. He is known as Faithful and True, he holds a sword and goes to battle with a robe dipped in the blood of his enemies as he fights for justice and wages war against evil.

He wants you to fight alongside him and the victory is already complete and sure, because the name He has tattooed on his leg tells us who He is : "KING OF KINGS and LORD OF LORDS".

This Jesus, the man from heaven wants to come to your home. The Bible says that his dwelling place now is to live "in your heart, by faith" as he gets you ready for an eternal home with him. I tell children Jesus wants to live in their hearts and they accept that in a simple way. Adults struggle with the physics of it. That's why Jesus said we must be childlike in our faith if we're ever going to see the kingdom of God.

I'm asking you now, before you close the book, to do

willingly in advance what you will have to do one day anyway. Simply believe, trust and declare the truth about Jesus while it has the power to save you, rather than condemn you. Jesus Christ is Lord! Tell him you will live to serve him. Offer back to him all your time, treasure and talents, and get ready for the adventure.

There will come a day when all creation will see him as he is now and acknowledge the truth about him. You will see him too, either when you die or at his return. The Bible doesn't warn us of that to scare us, but prepare us!

It says everyone will see him, even those who pierced him. There will be no denying his greatness and glory then. Those who have denied or blasphemed him will bend the knee and will have to speak the truth about the Only Perfect Man.

You, me, everyone who ever lived, will one day kneel in the dust from which we were made. He will separate the people, the lost and the found. All people will be gathered in like a great net full of fish and then the sorting will be quick and accurate.

People from every nation will be there to sing his praises. All mouths will acknowledge him – even those who never spoke in this life – shouting loud alongside the humble saint who suffered and was martyred for that truth, bowing down to declare it gladly. So too the devils, doubters and deniers will acknowledge what evil always wanted to suppress. The Truth will out, self-evident to the whole of creation.

When I saw this Jesus as he really is, as he is now, everything changed for me. Forever. You may not have any kind of vision like me. God had to show himself to me in this way because I was so hard and so far from him. But you may not need that kind of experience for Christ to change your life and your eternal destiny. It doesn't have to be the same. You don't have to go and borrow a mini or even make your way to the nearest church. You just have to recognize that Jesus' life, death and resurrection prove who he really is. Lord of all. Then you have to invite him to be Lord of you.

If you are ready to make that step you could choose to use the next few words as a prayer. But you could simply use your own words. God isn't interested in how intelligent you sound or if you use long or coherent words. He can see your heart.

As you are sitting reading this book, you can say something like this to God:

"I don't want to be a coal man any longer. I need your help, I've looked in the mirror of your perfection and I know I'm not the man I should be. I need your forgiveness. I need your grace and power to be who only you can make me. In my relationships, my stewardship, my failures, every facet, shape me, change me – from the inside out. Please will you forgive me, take me on and become Lord of my life today."

You can do it. Because Jesus can do it! He can do anything. The Bible says Christ in YOU is the hope of glory!

Because his blood stained a cross
One day every knee will bow
He was silent as a sheep before the shearers
So every tongue will confess

Because he was flogged, rejected, abandoned and mocked
Every knee will bow
He did not use his power for his own salvation, but ours
Every tongue will confess

Because his death paid a debt he did not owe, that we could never pay
Every knee! Your knee!
He wore a crown of thorns, now many crowns, tasted

death then spat it out
Every tongue! Yours and mine!

Because the eyes closed in death now blaze with living fire
My knee bows
Crushed for my iniquities, wounded for my transgressions, cut for my healing
My tongue confesses that
Jesus Christ is Lord!

Because he cried out, "It is finished!"
When I see him, I will know him,
because I will be like him – a Diamond Geezer.

Contact

To contact Anthony:
Call +44(0)161 434 5505
For more information go to:
www.diamondgeezers.org